NEW VEGETARIAN COOKING

120 FAST, FRESH, AND

FABULOUS RECIPES

ROSE ELLIOT

SIMON & SCHUSTER
NEW YORK   LONDON   TORONTO   SYDNEY

Food photography by Michael Paul

So many people have been involved with this book in one way or another and I would like to thank them all—Viv Bowler, Senior Commissioning Editor at BBC Worldwide, and my agent, Barbara Levy, for seeing and sharing my vision for the book and helping to make it a reality, for which the talents of Isobel Gillan, designer, and Michael Paul, photographer, were essential, and much appreciated and valued. The photographic shoots were a particular pleasure—I'd like to thank Louise Mackaness for preparing the food so well, Kumiko Ochiai for styling the shots (as well as making wonderful coffee and giving me tips on Japanese cooking), and Yuki Sugiura for helping at the shoots. A big thank you, too, to Sarah Miles, who not only kept everything running smoothly throughout the editorial process, but also posed for all the chapter-opener shots. You're a star, Sarah! I'd also like to thank Rachel Connolly for her thorough yet sensitive editing of the text, Kelly Davis for proofreading and Isobel McLean for indexing, Dr Jacqueline Stordy for information on omega-3 oils, Lyndel Costain for advice on nutrition, and the British Vegetarian Society for general information and advice. As ever, a huge thank you to my family and friends, who must feel as if they have lived with this book for months, and most of all to my husband, Robert, who really has, helping with shopping, tasting, doing the dishes, and being generally patient and supportive. Thank you Robert, thank you everyone. It was really appreciated.

Simon & Schuster
Rockefeller Center
1230 Avenue of the Americas
New York, NY 10020

For information regarding special discounts for bulk purchases,
please contact Simon & Schuster Special Sales at 1-800-456-6798
or business@simonandschuster.com
Designed by Isobel Gillan

Manufactured in Italy by LEGO SpA
10 9 8 7 6 5 4 3 2 1
Library of Congress Cataloging-in-Publication data is available.
ISBN 0-7432-6269-7

CONTENTS

WHY I'M A VEGETARIAN

TO VEGANS, VEGETARIANS, THOSE WHO COOK FOR THEM, AND WOULD-BE

VEGETARIANS EVERYWHERE, I DEDICATE THIS BOOK TO YOU.

People often say to me, "My family and I are meat-eaters but we love to eat vegetarian food and I do enjoy cooking from your books." They are really apologetic about the fact that they are not completely vegetarian, as if this would upset me. Actually I feel flattered and happy when a

meat-eater—or anyone else, for that matter—tells me that they find my books helpful. No one is excluded, as far as I'm concerned. I believe that choice of diet is a very individual matter and I have no desire to impose my own views on other people.

Having said that, our choice of food may be a personal one, but it's also an important one. More and more studies are showing that the food we eat has a direct impact on our health, which seems like common sense to me. And time and again, when the diets of the healthiest people have been analyzed, they have been found to contain plenty of pulses, whole grains, nuts, soy, fresh fruits and vegetables, herbs and spices—precisely the foods upon which a healthy vegetarian/vegan diet is based. Eating them is no hardship either, as I hope this book demonstrates.

So our choice of food can empower us physically, giving us better health, enhanced performance, more energy, and joie de vivre. It can empower us in other ways, too. What we eat, and in particular whether or not we choose to eat meat, has repercussions in many areas, from issues of animal welfare and ecological concerns to famine in developing countries. Unspeakably cruel practices are still the rule. According to the British Soil Association, only 0.3 percent of livestock is organically or compassionately raised. Meat production and over-fishing really harm the planet—the increasing destruction of the rainforests for grazing land, the plundering of the oceans, and global warming from methane emitted by livestock are all proof of that. And did you know that, according to statistics produced by leading academics, we could feed all the people in this world if we in the West became vegetarian—or, in fact, closer to vegan?

I find it immensely rewarding and inspiring to know that the food I choose to buy and eat can have a positive impact on my own health and well-being and that of my family, as well as that of the world we live in. It may be a drop in the ocean, but it all helps.

The best part is that it isn't that difficult. So much has changed since I first started writing books. Then I really had to work hard to persuade people that vegetarian food was good to eat. Today everyone knows it is. What is needed now is advice on becoming a healthy vegetarian or vegan, the essential facts on nutrition for all age groups, and how to create a balanced diet. My aim in writing this book is to give as complete a picture as possible of a vegetarian or vegan lifestyle. I've included information and tips I've gleaned as a lifelong vegetarian (now mostly vegan), followed by the recipes to put it all into practice. Knowing that we all have less and less time to spend preparing food, I was also determined that the recipes should be as quick and easy as possible, based on fresh ingredients and that, of course, they would taste fabulous—fast, fresh, and fabulous.

So I hope that, whether you're a vegetarian or a vegan, a meat-eater who enjoys a change sometimes, or someone who simply wants to cook tasty and healthy meals for vegetarian friends and family, you'll feel there's something here for you.

COOK'S NOTES

The ingredients you need are fully described and explained throughout the book and there are also hints on how to find suppliers at the back (see pages 188–189), so I hope you'll find everything clear and easy to follow. Many of the ingredients are easy to get just about anywhere; a few are less well known but are available in health food stores, ethnic grocery stores, and specialty markets, although they are beginning to creep onto the shelves of regular supermarkets.

All the recipes in this book list both American and metric measurements. Conversions are approximate and have been rounded up or down. In most of the recipes you can be fairly relaxed about measuring, but to be on the safe side it's always best to choose one set of measurements and stick with it, rather than mixing them.

If you have a fan-assisted oven, you need to reduce the temperatures as recommended by your oven manufacturer. On my oven this usually means reducing the heat by about two notches on the dial, so 350°F (180°C) becomes 325°F (160°C), and so on. In the few recipes in which eggs are used, they should be large, free-range, and preferably organic.

Australian cooks

Your tablespoons are equivalent to 4 teaspoons (20 ml) whereas ours are only 3 teaspoons (15 ml), so where tablespoons are given, please measure 3 teaspoons to get the correct amount.

American cooks

Although this book was originally written in the United Kingdom, the instructions and measurements, including liquids, have been adapted for the American kitchen.

BEING A HEALTHY VEGETARIAN OR VEGAN MEANS EATING A

BALANCED DIET THAT PROVIDES ALL THE NUTRIENTS NEEDED FOR ENERGY, GROWTH, REPAIR, MAINTENANCE, AND PROTECTION, IN ROUGHLY THE RIGHT PROPORTIONS. WE NEED PROTEIN, CARBOHYDRATES, VITAMINS, MINERALS, AND ESSENTIAL FATS—AND A VEGETARIAN OR VEGAN DIET CAN SUPPLY THEM ALL.

PROTEIN

Protein is essential for growth, maintenance, and repair of tissues, and for the healthy functioning of the body. The best sources of protein are:

■ nuts and seeds

■ beans and lentils

■ soy milk and soy yogurt

■ traditional protein products such as tofu, tempeh, and seitan

■ dairy products, such as milk, cheese, and yogurt

■ free-range eggs.

Certain grains, especially quinoa and amaranth, contain some protein though they are mainly carbohydrate (see page 110). Many foods, even potatoes, apples, and leaf vegetables, contain small amounts of protein.

All protein, whether of animal or vegetable origin, is made up of building blocks called amino acids, arranged in different patterns in different foods. When your body has unpicked the patterns it doesn't know whether these blocks have come from chickens, chickpeas, or chicory.

There are twenty of these amino acids. Our bodies can make some of them, but there are nine which it cannot make. These are called essential amino acids. Like meat and fish, all the protein foods mentioned above contain these essential amino acids, but the mix in animal proteins is closer to what our bodies want. The vegetable proteins are a little more erratic. Fortunately, the amino acids some foods lack, others can supply. Grains are rich in one of the essential amino acids, beans in another, so if you have, say, baked beans on toast, hummus and pita bread, or lentils and rice, you are getting the full complement. This mixing often happens naturally in a meal, but if it doesn't, your body can store unused amino acids for matching up later.

You can get all the protein you need from vegetable sources. The trick is to eat as wide a variety of these foods as possible and to resist the temptation to rely too much on dairy foods. That way you get the benefit of maximum nourishment for optimum health.

CARBOHYDRATE

Carbohydrate is our main source of energy, and is found in three forms:

■ simple sugars, found in fruits, milk, and all types of sugar

■ complex carbohydrates or starches, found in cereals and grains such as bread, rice, potatoes, and all other vegetables. Beans and lentils contain complex carbohydrate as well as protein.

■ fiber, now called non-starch polysaccharide (NSP), is the cellulose, tough cell walls, and gums in fruits, vegetables, and cereals. It's indigestible but vital to the healthy functioning of the gut.

Our bodies break carbohydrates down into simple sugars, which are then absorbed into the bloodstream, giving us energy. Generally, the more fibrous a carbohydrate, the more slowly it is broken down as the sugars separate from the fiber during digestion. This gives slow, sustained energy and it is one of the reasons why complex carbohydrates such as whole grains, vegetables, and pulses are so beneficial. Refined sugar and many products made from it are absorbed relatively quickly into the bloodstream, however, giving a quick "high" of energy, which is less sustained and means we may soon start looking for another energy boost.

So, while we need carbohydrates for energy, what we don't need is refined sugar, which has been described as "empty calories" because calories/energy are all it gives us.

Natural sweeteners are available that can be used instead of refined sugars (see *page 164*). I prefer to use these rather than artificial sweeteners.

The glycemic index

Foods containing carbohydrate register on the glycemic index (GI) according to how quickly they raise the blood glucose (sugar) level as they are broken down and digested. The more refined, sweet, and starchy the food, the higher it registers on the GI. It gives you a quick energy burst but triggers your system to release insulin rapidly and quickly store or use the blood glucose.

Foods containing little or no carbohydrate, such as meats, fish, fats, cheese, seeds, avocado, olives, and tofu don't have a GI rating. Most fruits have a low GI, with the exception of very sweet tropical fruits, such as pineapple, mango, and watermelon. While sugary and refined foods are generally high, beans and lentils are low, as are many whole grains, including oats, barley, buckwheat, and quinoa. Most white rice is high, though white basmati rice is medium (the same as brown basmati), especially if it's cooked slightly al dente.

Raw vegetables and most cooked vegetables are low, though mashed potato is high—in general, potatoes are lower when they're new, unpeeled, and slightly undercooked, or baked and eaten with their skins, but they're still on the high side and best eaten with pulses or lots of other vegetables to slow the absorption of carbohydrate. Sweet potatoes are lower than potatoes.

It's healthiest to eat foods with a low or medium glycemic index rating, but you don't need complicated tables and calculators to work this out. Just remember to stick to whole, unrefined cereals, pulses, tofu, vegetables, nuts, yogurt, and fruits most of the time. And if you eat any foods with a high rating on the GI, you can lessen the effect by eating them with something with a low GI rating, like yogurt, pulses, pasta, fruit, or suitable whole grains.

Adding fresh lemon juice (or vinegar) also significantly lowers the GI rating of a food; the reasons are not clear, but it is thought that it may have something to do with the acidic qualities of the lemon juice, which is great, because a dash of lemon enhances the flavor of so many foods, as well as providing some vitamin C and other body-protecting antioxidants.

MINERALS AND VITAMINS

Most minerals and vitamins pose no problems for vegetarians or vegans; indeed our diet is typically richer in vitamins A and C, B vitamins biotin, pantothenic acid, folate and B_6, and magnesium, than a meat diet. We do need to look at iron, calcium, vitamin B_{12}, vitamin D, riboflavin (B_2), and iodine.

Iron

We need iron for healthy blood and energy, and since meat is a prime source, people often worry about how vegetarians and vegans can get enough. However, perhaps surprisingly, studies have consistently shown that vegetarians and vegans are no more likely to suffer from lack of iron than meat eaters. The following are good sources of iron:

- grains and grain products such as whole wheat bread and pasta, millet, quinoa
- fortified breakfast cereals

- dried fruits, especially apricots, figs, and peaches
- nuts and seeds, especially almonds, pistachio nuts, and pumpkin seeds
- lentils, peas, and beans, including soy products
- molasses
- green leaf vegetables.

A vital point is that we absorb more iron when we eat foods containing it alongside a good source of vitamin C, such as lemon juice, fresh fruits, or vegetable juices. A balanced vegetarian or vegan diet, planned along the lines suggested in this book, includes sufficient iron.

Calcium

Calcium is essential for healthy bones and teeth. Most people know it's found in dairy produce, but there are also some rich vegetable sources. One cup of cooked kale contains about the same amount of usable calcium as ¾ cup (175 ml) of milk. Calcium is found in:

- milk, yogurt, and cheese
- green leaf vegetables, such as purple sprouting broccoli, kale, collard greens, and watercress
- white flour and white bread that has been fortified with calcium
- dried fruits, especially figs
- fortified soy milk, and tofu prepared with calcium sulfate—check the label
- blackstrap molasses
- tap water in hard water areas and some bottled mineral waters—read the label.

The calcium issue is a complex one because a number of factors can affect our ability to absorb and retain it. As calcium is needed by the body to process protein, some apparently rich sources of calcium aren't that effective if they're also high in protein. That's one of the reasons why I think it's a mistake for vegetarians to rely too much on dairy foods. It's important to eat other good sources of calcium, as listed above, regularly. And for vegans, these are essential and need to be eaten daily.

Healthy bones depend on more than just calcium. Vitamin D is essential for the full absorption of calcium (see below) and so is magnesium, which is a constituent of chlorophyll and therefore abundant in green leaf vegetables—if you eat kale, collard greens, or watercress, you get both calcium and magnesium. Other good sources of magnesium are whole grains, wheat germ, molasses, seeds, nuts, apples, and figs. And don't forget that weight-bearing exercise, such as walking, running, and dancing (though not swimming), is also important for building and keeping healthy bones.

We also need to reduce the amount of calcium our bodies lose. Cutting down on caffeine and alcohol can definitely help here, as can eating foods that contain the trace mineral boron—apples, grapes, pears, prunes, dates, raisins, almonds, peanuts, and hazelnuts.

Vitamin B_{12}

This is a vital vitamin, but only very tiny amounts are needed. Vegetarians can get this vitamin from dairy foods and free-range eggs. If you're a vegan, you just need to make sure that, preferably daily, you eat foods such as soy milk, yeast extract, veggie burgers, and breakfast cereals that have been fortified with B_{12} (read the label). Alternatively, you can always take a supplement.

Vitamin D

Vitamin D is made by the action of the sun on the skin. It's also in milk, cheese, and butter and is added to most margarines, including soy margarine.

Healthy adult vegetarians and vegans can usually get enough from these sources, but the very young, the very old, and those who spend most of their time indoors would be well advised to take a vitamin D supplement, especially if they're eating little or no dairy produce or margarine.

Riboflavin (B_2)

We need this for the release of energy from food and for healthy skin, eyes, and hair. For most people, milk and cheese are important sources of riboflavin, so vegans and vegetarians eating little dairy produce need to make sure they include other good sources, such as:

- almonds
- yeast and yeast extract
- wheat germ and quinoa
- soybeans
- avocado
- fortified breakfast cereals
- soy milk.

Iodine

We need iodine for the healthy functioning of the thyroid gland. Most people in the US, including vegetarians, get about half their daily iodine from dairy products. Vegans and vegetarians eating only a little dairy produce can add iodine to their diet by eating seaweed two or three times a week (see page 122). You don't need much iodine, and it's important not to take too much—4 ounces (115 g) dried hijiki or ½ ounce (15 g) dried kombu provide a year's supply for one person. Nori doesn't contain much iodine and you can eat several sheets a day without worrying about overdosing. Using an unrefined salt (see page 113) will supply a balanced source of iodine as well as some of the trace minerals lacking in other salts.

ESSENTIAL FATS

All fats contain fatty acids. These may be saturated like coconut oil, butter, and animal fats, monounsaturated like olive oil, or polyunsaturated like sunflower, safflower, and soybean oil. Our bodies can make saturated and monounsaturated fats, but there are two polyunsaturated fats (PUFAs) they can't make—linoleic acid and alpha-linolenic acid, parents of the omega-6 and omega-3 oils. So these are called essential fatty acids and they have to be provided in our food.

Linoleic acid and omega-6 oils are found in vegetables, fruits, nuts, grains, and seeds; oils made from corn, sunflower, soy, evening primrose, pumpkin, and wheat germ are also good sources.

Alpha-linolenic acid and omega-3 oils are found in fish oils, eggs, and blue-green algae, which presumably is where the fish get it from originally. These are called "long chain" omega-3 oils. "Short chain" omega-3 oils are found in flaxseed, walnut,

soybean, and canola oils, green leaf vegetables, grains, algae called spirulina, and nori seaweed. You can also buy eggs which have been enriched with omega-3 by feeding the hens a supplement made from seeds or algae. Some of the vegetable sources of omega-3 are very rich. Flaxseed oil, for instance, contributes twice as much omega-3 as fish oil, but it's not clear how efficiently our bodies can convert the short chain omega-3s into the long chain ones it needs.

This fat question is quite complex because it's not just our intake of the different fats but the proportions that are important. For instance, if we eat a lot of saturated fat (in milk, cheese, cream, and eggs) we may impair our body's ability to process omega-6 and omega-3 oils, another reason for not eating too much dairy. In addition, our utilization of omega-3 may be hindered if we have too high a level of omega-6. Because of all these factors, we now have a much higher proportion of omega-6 to omega-3 acids in our bodies than ever before. Some nutritional therapists are worried about this and claim it is the cause of all kinds of aches and pains (such as premenstrual syndrome). Some even link it with cancer.

Studies have shown that vegetarians and vegans take in considerably more omega-6 than do omnivores, though they absorb roughly the same levels of omega-3. So, in spite of the perceived healthiness of sunflower oil, vegetarians and vegans can achieve a better balance by using more omega-3 oils—canola instead of sunflower, safflower, or corn oil; walnut or cold-pressed canola oil on salads as a change from olive oil; and a tablespoon of cold-pressed flaxseed oil or a rounded tablespoon of finely ground flaxseeds every day. To be on the safe side, I also recommend a daily supplement of the algae-derived omega-3 oils (*see page 189*).

TRANS-FATTY ACIDS

Trans-fatty acids are formed when unsaturated fats, such as vegetable oils, are hydrogenated to solidify them, as in margarine and cooking fats. They are thus present in most store-bought cakes, cookies, pastries, fried foods, and in many ready meals and hard margarines. Trans-fats are of concern because they may interfere with the body's ability to utilize the omega-3 oils that have been found to be important for brain function, healthy blood, and a healthy heart. I particularly worry about the effect on children of all the trans-fats they eat in store-bought fast foods, cookies, and other snack foods. They need good sources of omega-3 oils to compensate and ensure healthy growth and brain development.

Trans-fats, like saturated fats, can also raise cholesterol levels.

CREATING A BALANCED DIET

The following demonstrates a good intake of vegetarian or vegan nutrients over a day. You don't have to stick to this plan rigidly; use it as a general guide for a balanced and healthy diet.

A "portion" consists of, for example, a slice of bread, an apple, a glass of milk, or two tablespoons of cooked beans or grains. A typical serving at a meal might well consist of more than one portion.

Fruit and vegetables
- 5 portions daily, at least—the more the better. Fresh, frozen, juiced, canned, or dried fruits and vegetables—seaweeds, if you like them—supply vitamins, minerals, and fiber.

Milk and soy milk foods
- 2–3 portions daily. Can be cows' milk and foods, or soy milk and foods.

Alternatives to meat and fish
- 2–3 portions daily. Include a wide variety of beans and lentils, nuts, seeds, eggs, and traditional protein foods such as tofu, tempeh, and seitan (see page 140).

Bread, cereals, potatoes
- 5 or more portions daily. Use the whole grain versions as often as possible, and try some unusual grains such as millet, sorghum, buckwheat, amaranth, barley, and quinoa.

Essential fats
- 1 tablespoon of finely ground flaxseed, or 1–2 tablespoons of flaxseed oil or canola oil daily; walnuts or walnut oil regularly.

PLANNING HEALTHY MEALS

It's easy to plan healthy, balanced meals if you use the formula: Protein, carbohydrate, fruits, and vegetables. Choose your protein (beans, lentils, nuts, seeds, tofu, tempeh, seitan, soy or cows' milk and yogurt, cheese, eggs), your carbohydrate (rice, bread, pasta, potatoes), then add fruits and vegetables to make an appetizing meal. Base your meals on what I call this "healthy trinity" and your diet will automatically be balanced.

At its simplest, this could be baked beans (protein), toast (carbohydrate), and an apple or salad on the side (fruits and vegetables). As beans and lentils are half protein, half carbohydrate, when using them as protein I often boost them by adding a few nuts or seeds or some yogurt— so in the previous example, you could have yogurt or a piece of cheese with the apple or salad. Of course, some dishes, such as Moroccan Chickpea Casserole (see *page 117*), contain all the elements (in this case, chickpeas for protein, rice for carbohydrate, with eggplant, onion, bell

peppers, and garlic for the vegetables) to make life really easy. In any case, planning meals is fun if you build them up in this way.

Here are some more examples:

Protein	Carbohydrate	Fruit and vegetables
Breakfasts		
Soy or dairy yogurt	Muesli or oatbran	Dried or fresh fruit
Scrambled egg or tofu	whole wheat or rye toast	Broiled tomatoes
		Fruit or vegetable juice
Lunches and evening meals		
Hummus	Pita bread	Tomato and lettuce
Ginger-marinated tofu	Cooked noodles	Stir-fried vegetables
Dal	Brown basmati rice	Spiced spinach, tomatoes, and coriander
Chili bean dish	Baked potato	Green salad or fruit salad

GET SLIM AND STAY SLIM DO YOU WANT TO REACH YOUR IDEAL WEIGHT AND STAY THERE WITHOUT CONSTANT DIETING; TO FEEL HEALTHY AND FULL OF ENERGY EVERY DAY WITHOUT BLOATING, HEADACHES, ASSORTED ACHES AND PAINS? TO LOOK AND FEEL YOUNGER AND FITTER FOR LONGER?

Of course, what we all want is a miracle diet that will enable us to get to our desired weight rapidly and then stay there forever. I wish I could offer you exactly that, but unfortunately it doesn't exist.

What I can give you, however, is a workable way of getting to your perfect weight and then staying there. Imagine what it would be like for the weight to drop off you steadily while you feel inwardly at peace and not always craving foods or drinks that you can't have; to have the confidence that comes from knowing you're looking your very best, and that your eating is under control, and you'll never again have to go on a diet. It can be done; the way of life described in this book and the recipes will make that possible.

The first thing to do is to stop thinking of a diet as a quick fix to help you reach a certain weight as fast as you can, so that you can then stop the diet and eat "normally." I've finally realized that as long as you go on thinking that way, you're doomed to failure, because if you're "on" a diet, you can easily fall "off" a diet. It need not be like that. Here is another approach.

Discover your "trigger foods"

Many people who try to stick to a diet have certain foods that cause them to start binging. These foods could be anything—bread, cookies, potato chips, potatoes, nuts, cream cakes, candy, chocolate. The way to find out is to keep a food diary—write down everything you eat and drink for a week. You'll soon find the guilty foods. I recommend the book *Stop Bingeing!* by Lee Janogly (see *page 189*) for more about trigger foods and some very sensible dieting advice.

Always eat a good breakfast, including protein, a little carbohydrate, and if possible a little fruit, fruit juice, or a few vegetables, and never go longer than three hours without eating.

Find the breakfast which works for you and make time in the morning to eat it. Remember, protein, a little carbohydrate, and some fruit or vegetables (see *opposite for ideas*). Just do it!

Don't let your blood sugar and your energy dip too much by going longer than three hours without food. Have something light and nourishing if you can't have a proper meal: low-fat or soy yogurt, an apple, a mug of Golden Lentil Soup (see *page 82*), some drained, canned chickpeas or red kidney beans, or a small can of baked beans or green beans. Get into the habit of thinking ahead and carrying a little low-fat, nourishing food with you when you're out and about.

Be sure to have a good quantity of protein and a little carbohydrate with every meal, plus plenty of fruits and vegetables.

If you haven't eaten like this before, you'll be amazed how much more energy you will have when you do. While you're wanting to lose weight it's helpful to concentrate on high-protein, low-fat vegetarian foods. These are all the soy foods—soy milk, soy yogurt (plain is best, sweetened, if you like, with a tablespoon of sugarless fruit jelly or some organic dried apricot purée), tofu, and tempeh—as well as seitan (made from wheat gluten, a wheat product I really recommend) and, if you eat dairy, low-fat milk, yogurt, and cottage cheese. Have any of these with plenty of vegetables and a little carbohydrate such as some brown rice, millet, buckwheat, quinoa, as well as beans or lentils, which supply both carbohydrate and extra protein.

Eat foods with a low GI rating

This basically means sticking to the foods that keep your blood sugar steady and help regulate your appetite and so keep your weight in check. There's more about the glycemic index on page 9. The secret is to make foods with a low GI rating the

mainstay of your diet. Because these are the healthy foods upon which this book is based, the vast majority of recipes have a low GI rating, so you can use them while you're losing weight, and then continue to enjoy them without piling on the pounds again.

Sugar and sugary drinks both have a high GI rating and won't help you to lose weight; in fact they'll do the opposite. Of course, the odd drink or spoonful of sugar won't hurt—unless these are your trigger foods. But for health and for dieting, they're best reserved for the occasional treat.

There are some natural sweeteners that won't send your blood sugar racing (see page 164). Once you've reached the weight you want to be, it's fine to use these sometimes—unless the very taste of something sweet is enough to start you eating unhealthily again—but your best policy is to train your tastebuds not to want tastes that are too sweet. This takes time, but you'll get to the stage when a salad of grated raw beets tastes as sweet as a sugary dessert.

Eat normally but be choosy

I don't recommend using "diet" foods. I think the psychology behind them is wrong and the food doesn't taste good. It's much better to choose dishes which are naturally low in fat and calories. Because this book is about healthy vegetarian eating, the majority of the dishes in it are ones you can happily eat—and share with others— while you're dieting. Keep your portions quite modest and fill up on vegetables and salads, with low-fat yogurt, soy yogurt, fresh fruits, or fruit salad, or a simple dessert such as Apricot and Orange Fool with Pistachios (see page 166).

When it comes to special occasions, as long as you keep off your trigger foods, I think it's better to have a smaller portion of a regular, rich dish, than make a "dieter's" version which will inevitably not be as good and will make you feel deprived. So, when you have to have something rich, just eat a little, and make up the space on your plate with plenty of vegetables or salad if it's savory, or fresh fruit or plain yogurt if it's sweet.

Follow these guidelines, get a little exercise every day, even if it's just a 20-minute walk, and enjoy trying the recipes in this book, which will help get you slim and keep you healthy. Gradually, you'll find you get on an even keel with your eating. Your weight will come down, your energy and sense of well-being will increase, you'll be looking and feeling like a million dollars and, most of all, you'll be liberated from dieting for ever.

A few dieting tips

- Eat green beans. According to leading herbalist Jill Davies, these flush toxins from the body and help to keep blood sugar levels steady so you don't get energy dips.

- Drink plenty of water, 1 2 quarts every day isn't too much.
- Avoid refined foods, sugar, cakes, cookies, alcohol, and soda pop. That way you will bypass many food additives such as thickeners, emul- sifiers, artificial sweeteners, colorings, flavorings, and unhealthy fats that your body doesn't need. You'll also find that whole grain cereals, fruits, or yogurts are much more satisfying.
- Wean yourself off coffee, you'll feel much better. Do it over a weekend and take painkillers if you get a withdrawal headache. You can still have decaffeinated coffee sometimes, and plenty of herb teas and "coffee" made from cereal grains.
- Restrict fried foods to the occasional treat; eat them with steamed vegetables or salad.

WHEAT AND DAIRY It's become quite a fashion fad to stop eating wheat and dairy foods, and some people certainly feel better when they give up these products. The trouble is that most people eat so much of them and, in the case of wheat, in a refined form, such as white bread, pasta, cookies, puff and phyllo pastries, couscous, etc. This is especially true of vegetarians, as many "vegetarian options" feature the ingredients I've just mentioned. When you're overexposed to a food you may overrely on it and so upset the healthy balance of your diet, which could lead to overeating, lethargy, bloating, and tiredness.

An important key to good health is to eat a wide range of foods, so it can be very helpful to take a break from wheat and dairy, or at least to cut down and try a variety of other nutritious foods instead. There are plenty to choose from and you'll find lots of recipes for them in this book.

If you suspect food intolerance, always seek advice from your doctor and/or nutritionist.

EATING FOR TWO
VEGETARIANS AND VEGANS REALLY CAN PRODUCE PERFECT, HEALTHY CHILDREN. BABIES ARE BEING BORN TO FOURTH- AND FIFTH-GENERATION VEGETARIANS AND VEGANS IN THE UNITED STATES NOW, AND ALL AROUND THE WORLD WHOLE CULTURES HAVE BEEN VEGETARIAN FOR THOUSANDS OF YEARS.

If you're planning to have a baby in the near future, you can give it the best possible start by preparing in advance. As some forms of the contraceptive pill may reduce the absorption of nutrients, it's a good idea to check with your doctor or use another form of contraception while you prepare for pregnancy; you would also be wise to cut back on alcohol and caffeine.

Build up your health and vitality with a good diet, as described on pages 8–14. In particular, make sure your intake of vitamins B_{12} and D is adequate (*see page 11*), and that you're getting enough of the other B vitamins, especially folic acid, as well as iron and vitamin E, by eating plenty of dark-green leaf vegetables (at least one good serving every day), yeast extract, pulses, and whole grain cereals, and have a good portion of protein at every meal. Include some omega-3 oils every day, such as flaxseed or their oil, cold-pressed canola oil, walnuts, and walnut oil, and consider taking a vegetarian omega-3 supplement (*see page 189*) or including omega-3 enriched eggs in your diet. Eat lots of fruit (especially oranges and orange juice for the folic acid) and vegetables, and drink plenty of water.

Because it's such an important vitamin for pregnancy, health experts advise that, in addition to a healthy diet, it's important to take a 400 mcg supplement of folic acid while you're preparing for pregnancy and right up until you're twelve weeks pregnant.

If you've been eating as described, you'll be off to a really good start and can continue in the same way once you're pregnant. Even if you haven't been able to prepare, it's never too late, and pregnancy is a great time to improve your diet, to nurture yourself and the new life growing inside you. You'll need slightly increased amounts of vitamins A, B_1, B_2, C, D, and folic acid than usual throughout your pregnancy, but your requirement for minerals such as iron, calcium, magnesium, zinc, and iodine doesn't change, because your body is working more efficiently and absorbing more nutrients. If you think you may not be getting all the nutrients you need, it might be wise to take a vitamin supplement. Choose one that has been specially formulated for pregnancy, without too much vitamin A, as this has been associated with birth defects. Check with your prenatal clinic or pharmacist if in doubt.

You don't need to eat a lot more when you're pregnant, just an extra 200 calories during the last three months, easily supplied by a nutritious snack such as those described opposite. It's when the baby has arrived and you're breastfeeding that you really have to "eat for two," because then you need 500 extra calories. If you don't eat enough, you may not produce as much milk. You also need to make sure you drink plenty of water. At first it's hard even to find time to make meals for yourself, so having several good-quality snacks instead could be more practical.

Healthy snacks

- Light and Creamy Hummus (see *page 86*) with raw vegetables or whole wheat bread.
- Whole wheat watercress sandwiches with yeast extract.
- A bowl of Golden Lentil Soup (see *page 82*).
- A handful of nuts and seeds with dried fruits.
- A piece of Sticky Parkin (see *page 182*).
- An almond or banana smoothie (see *page 118*), perhaps with an extra spoonful of molasses.
- Some soy or dairy yogurt with a chopped banana and a sprinkling of chopped almonds or wheat germ.
- A bowl of granola, muesli, or Iron-rich Breakfast Mix (see *page 118*), with milk or soy milk.
- Whole grain nut butter sandwiches, perhaps with some yeast extract and salad.
- Lentil Dal (see *page 105*) with brown rice.
- A bowl of creamy oatmeal (made with half water, half milk), topped with flaked, chopped or ground almonds or hazelnuts.
- Brown rice with cooked spinach and onion.
- A bowl of Dried Fruit Compote (see *page 168*) with molasses and pistachio nuts.

What to avoid

All the experts advise pregnant women to avoid the following foods during pregnancy because of the risk of salmonella or listeria:

- All unpasteurized milk (cow, sheep, or goat)
- Soft-serve ice cream
- Raw egg (watch out for it in desserts or homemade mayonnaise)
- Vegetable pâté (unless cooked or pasteurized)
- Soft cheeses such as blue cheese, Gruyère, Camembert, brie, feta, and the Mexican queso blanco and queso fresco.

In addition, prepared salads need to be washed thoroughly before eating, while heat and serve meals must be thoroughly heated until really hot.

Iron-boosting ideas

If you need to increase your iron level, here are some ideas. A week or so of concentrated "iron snacking" can really help.

- Choose an iron-rich grain such as millet or whole wheat pasta, rather than rice; almonds, preferably blanched (the skins can hinder iron absorption); and pumpkin seeds (pepitas). Try eating the Iron-rich Breakfast Mix (see *page 118*) which can supply up to 25 mg of iron.
- Concentrate on pulses that are highest in iron—lentils and soybeans—cooked or sprouted (see *page 67*). Add a little soy flour to sauces and casseroles, and sprinkle nutritional yeast flakes over your food.
- Eat plenty of dark-green leafy vegetables: 1 pound (450 g) spinach, collard greens, or kale, sautéed with an onion and garlic in oil, then served on brown rice, is an iron-rich meal, or you could prepare 2¼ pounds (1 kg) organic carrots juiced with 8 ounces (225 g) parsley stalks and leaves—it's quite strong, so you might want to juice it in two or three batches.
- Snack on dried fruit, and try the iron-rich variation of the Dried Fruit Compote (see *page 168*). Eaten in small servings throughout the day, this can provide up to 20 mg of iron. You can also drink prune juice, which is much tastier than it sounds (especially with a shot of club soda), or use it to moisten your breakfast cereal (it's good with muesli and granola).
- Take some blackstrap molasses daily, straight from the spoon or dissolved in milk, mixed with a little honey, or in desserts.

NURTURING THE NEXT GENERATION RESEARCH HAS SHOWN THAT A WELL-BALANCED VEGETARIAN DIET IS HEALTHY FOR BABIES AND CHILDREN AND PROVIDES ALL THE NOURISHMENT THEY NEED. THIS IS NOW WIDELY ACKNOWLEDGED AMONG HEALTH PROFESSIONALS, INCLUDING THE AMERICAN DIETETIC ASSOCIATION.

BABIES

As well as being a healthy choice, it's quite safe to bring a child up as a vegetarian or vegan. Indeed, I have myself brought up three healthy daughters on a vegetarian diet. The important thing is to make sure you include plenty of nutrient-rich foods in their diet. Where concern has been expressed over the growth of babies and children on vegetarian-type diets, they were in communities following very restrictive, rather than typical, vegetarian or vegan diets.

There's no doubt that breastfeeding your baby, even if it's only for a few weeks, will give

him or her the best possible start. However, if you don't want to, or can't breastfeed your baby, there are formula milks which are fine for vegetarians. If you're vegan, you may wonder about the advisability of using soy-based formula, since some concern has been expressed regarding their safety. However, studies on people who were raised on soy formula as babies twenty years ago have shown them to have had no adverse effects overall (apart from allergic reactions in susceptible infants), and there have been literally hundreds of studies demonstrating the positive effects of soybeans generally.

Weaning

Weaning is the process of gradually introducing solid foods into a milk diet until baby is eating normal meals. You can start the weaning process by offering some little tastes of solid food once your baby is four months old. Over the weeks, gradually increase the amount of solid food so that the baby is taking less and less milk; by about eight months most babies will eat some solids three times a day before their milk feeds, which remain very important both nutritionally and emotionally. Eventually, they will drop the milk feeds one by one, so that by the time they're a year old they will be eating three meals a day, though many babies continue with a nighttime feed or formula for at least another year.

Start with half a teaspoon of your chosen food, either before or after a milk feed, at lunchtime or in the evening, whichever is the most convenient. Good foods with which to start the weaning process are mashed ripe banana, peach, mango, papaya, or avocado; puréed cooked apple, carrot or sweet potato; or a thin gruel made from baby rice (choose a plain, unsweetened one), flaked millet, or quinoa.

As your baby takes more solid food and less milk, you will need to add other nutritious ingredients to the basic fruit and vegetable purées. Puréed lentils (made from split red lentils, without spices or seasoning but with a little walnut, flaxseed, or canola oil for extra energy and omega-3 oils) are perfect; so are puréed tofu, live soy yogurt, very finely ground nuts and seeds (ground almonds are good), tahini or homemade, unsalted hummus, organic nut butters, nutritional yeast (from health food stores), beans (including Boston-style baked beans without added salt, sugar, or sweeteners), and some low-salt yeast extract fortified with vitamin B_{12}. If you're bringing your baby up as a vegan, make sure you include vitamin B_{12}-fortified foods and ask your doctor about a vitamin D supplement.

Babies need small, frequent meals of concentrated nutrients. Avoid too many watery or bulky foods and be sure to include the concentrated sources of energy and protein described above. Also include iron-rich foods daily, such as soaked and puréed dried apricots, fortified cereals, molasses, red lentils, beans, and dark green vegetables. Give baby these foods alongside fruit and vegetable juices, which are good sources of vitamin C, for maximum iron absorption.

Baby food notes and tips

- For the first six months, don't give baby wheat, nuts, seeds, eggs, citrus fruits, or cows' milk, and no dairy foods at all if there is a history of allergies in your family. Ask your pediatrician for advice.

- Mix nutritious but strong-tasting vegetables, including broccoli and kale or collards, with a sweet vegetable such as sweet potato, squash, or parsnip. The baby will love them that way.

- Cook tiny pasta shapes and mash them with vegetables and a protein ingredient for a balanced meal.

- Increase the variety of foods, mashing or sieving family foods for your baby to share, as long as they don't contain added salt (which can put a strain on the baby's kidneys), or too much spice or any other unsuitable foods.

- Never give whole nuts to any child under five and if there is a history of allergies in your family, avoid nuts for the first three years.

- Avoid foods containing sugar, including zwieback and sweet cookies.

- The manufacturers of textured vegetable proteins and similar meat substitutes recommend that they are not given to children aged under two years. It's my view that cooked beans, lentils, grains, tofu, tempeh, and seitan are preferable to these at any age.

- Continue breastfeeding or giving infant formula until baby is one year old. Whole cows' milk can then be introduced. Don't give lowfat or nonfat milk to children under two years, and don't give skim milk to children under five. If you're using soy milk instead of cows' milk, it's best to choose one that has been fortified with calcium and vitamins B_{12} and D, or use a soy baby formula.

CHILDREN AND TEENAGERS

The foods described for weaning your baby—pulses, whole grains, and vegetables, enriched with protein, and in some cases ingredients high in fat—continue to offer the best nourishment for a growing child. Many of the recipes in this book are suitable for children. I am all in favor of shared meals, enjoyed by children and adults alike. Favorite entrées in my family include Best-ever Chili (see page 99), served with cooked rice or baked potatoes (if you use rice, any leftover chili and rice can be mashed together, formed into burger shapes, rolled in dry crumbs and fried to make a meal for the children another day); Lentil and Cumin Cakes with Minty Raita (see page 90); Spaghetti with Red Hot Sauce (see page 63); and Khitchari (see page 133).

It's far better for your children if you limit storebought cookies and cakes, sweetened drinks and soda pop, and salty snacks such as potato chips. It helps to be prepared, with plenty of good foods available for snacks (see opposite). However, try not to get too tense about the situation; remember, a child who has a basically healthy diet, as described in this book, can withstand a little "junk" food now and then.

OLDER CHILDREN

As children get older, especially if they're lively and love sports, their need for high-energy foods will increase. The answer, strange as it may seem, is the same as that described for healthy weaning and toddler food (both are periods of fast growth and high energy output). Keep to the healthy formula of carbohydrate, protein, and fruits or vegetables, as described on page 14, boosted with foods which are energy- and nutrient-rich.

Nuts and seeds are excellent for this. They can be eaten whole, roasted, tossed in soy sauce, then crisped under the broiler or in the oven, or ground and sprinkled over breakfast cereals, salads, cooked grains and vegetables, stir-frys and pasta dishes, stirred into shakes, or eaten as snacks. Tahini, peanut butter, or the more unusual and delectable almond, walnut, or hazelnut butters found in health food stores, can be spread on bread, toast, and crispbreads, or drizzled over chopped banana or Dried Fruit Compote (see page 168). Light and Creamy Hummus (see page 86), rich with tahini, is a wonderfully healthy spread and dip for snacking, and is also great poured over baked potatoes.

Dried fruits are a good concentrated sugar source and contain some B vitamins, iron, and calcium. They can be added to cereals or flapjacks (see page 179) or fruit breads, soaked and made into desserts. Of course they are a handy snack on their own, perhaps with nuts and seeds.

It's also useful to have a supply of canned or cooked beans and cooked brown rice for instant healthy snacking. Heated—or eaten cold as a salad—and served with some chopped avocado or a swirl of olive oil (or cold-pressed flaxseed or canola oil for their omega-3 content), they're very filling and nutritious. If getting enough calories is a problem, these good-quality oils can be sprinkled over almost anything.

Tofu, tempeh, and seitan are particularly good foods for this age group, too, because of their high protein content. They can be simply fried and served on whole wheat bread, packed into hamburger or kaiser rolls or inside pita pockets. Try them with Quick and Easy Peanut Sauce (see page 146) for even more protein and extra nourishment.

Healthy snacks for children

- A healthy dip such as Light and Creamy Hummus (see *page 86*), guacamole, or one of the other dips on pages 86–87, with ready-prepared raw vegetables, or rye or wheat bread fingers for dipping.
- Fresh fruits.
- A handful of raisins or other dried fruits.
- Nuts for children over five years.
- Cubes of cheese or marinated tofu.
- Oatcakes or rice cakes, toast or sandwiches, with nut butters, tahini, miso, yeast extract, tofu spread, all-fruit jelly or apricot purée (see *page 168*).
- A handful of drained, cooked chickpeas or red kidney beans.
- Tempeh Burgers (see *page 151*).
- Little Provençal Pancakes (see *page 102*) with tomato ketchup (choose a healthy one) or maple or agave syrup, or all-fruit jelly.
- A slice of Sticky Date Bread (see *page 183*) or Sticky Parkin (see *page 182*).
- A bowl of cereal with cows' or soy milk.
- A smoothie (see *page 118*).
- Baked potato with a spoonful of Light and Creamy Hummus (see *page 86*) or some grated cheese.
- Water, or real fruit juice diluted with water.

Daily servings for children (1–5 years)

This is just a guide—every child is different, and the servings should be adapted according to the age and needs of the individual child.

- Grains and cereals: 4–5 servings, including whole grain bread, rice, pasta, breakfast cereals, and potatoes.
- Pulses, nuts, seeds: 1–2 servings, including nut butters, tahini, lentils, and mashed beans.
- Dairy or soy: 3 servings, including milk, cheese, hard-boiled, free-range eggs, yogurt, fortified soy milk, and tofu.
- Vegetables: 2–3 servings, preferably including green leaf vegetables.
- Fruit: 1–3 servings, with dried fruits, at least once every few days.

ORGANICS FOR CHILDREN The effects of chemical residues from artificial fertilizers, pesticides, and other sprays used on nonorganic food is greater on children because of their smaller body weight and immature, developing systems. We do not know what long-term damage these, or genetically modified ingredients, may do, but I think it's worth paying a little extra for organic produce for peace of mind. By doing so, you also avoid hydrogenated fats and, by supporting organic producers, help to promote farming methods that benefit the environment.

LOOK YOUNGER, LIVE LONGER IF YOU WANT TO FIND THE KEY TO LOOKING YOUNGER AND LIVING LONGER, YOU CAN DO NO BETTER THAN STUDY THE DIET AND LIFESTYLE OF THE PEOPLE OF THE JAPANESE ISLANDS OF OKINAWA, WHERE THERE ARE MORE CENTENARIANS THAN ANYWHERE ELSE IN THE WORLD, AND WHERE THE PEOPLE STAY HAPPY AND ACTIVE THROUGHOUT THEIR LIVES.

Okinawa is an archipelago of 161 islands, stretching for 800 miles (1300km) between the Japanese main islands and Taiwan. It is also the home of the longest-lived people in the world, people who seem to have beaten the aging process, for whom heart disease is minimal, breast cancer so rare that screening is unnecessary, and where most men have never heard of prostate cancer. In fact, in Okinawa, the three leading killers in the West—heart disease, stroke, and cancer—occur with the lowest frequency in the world, and dementia rates among the elderly are markedly lower than in the United States and elsewhere in Japan. To quote from *The Okinawa Way* by Bradley Willcox, M.D., Craig Willcox, Ph.D., and Makoto Suzuki, M.D., describing what doctors learned from a twenty-five-year study of these people, the centenarians of Okinawa "have slim, lithe bodies, sharp clear eyes, quick wits, passionate interests, and the kind of Shangri-la glow that we all covet."

So what is their secret? As you might expect, there are a number of lifestyle factors, including their Eastern tradition and wisdom, spiritual beliefs, supportive community, regular exercise and diet, which undoubtedly contribute to the health and longevity of the Okinawans. Here, I'm going to concentrate on their diet and what it can show us about eating for health and longevity.

One of the most striking things about the Okinawan diet is the amount of complex carbohydrates (whole grains and grain products) and fresh vegetables of all kinds that it contains—a staggering 7–13 servings of each group every day! In addition to this, they eat 2–4 servings of fruit, 2–4 servings of pulses and soy products, especially tofu, small quantities of seaweed, small amounts of oil, and a wide variety of herbs and spices each day. They consume minimal amounts of dairy foods, which, combined with seaweed, makes up just 2 percent of their diet. They also eat 1–3 servings of fish and other omega-3-rich foods every day, and occasionally pork. Their total intake of fats is only 24 percent, compared with around 40 percent in the United States, and their main cooking oil is cold-pressed canola oil.

Apart from the fish and occasional pork, this diet plan is remarkably similar to that of a healthy vegetarian—and, in particular, vegan—diet. This may explain why vegetarians and vegans share the same low rates for heart disease and some cancers as the Okinawans. So, you're off to an excellent start if you follow these guidelines:

- Eat plenty of fruits and vegetables. You don't have to chew your way through massive salads. Make quick, easy-to-eat soups and casseroles, or invest in a good-quality juicer.
- Include soy foods, such as calcium-fortified tofu, soy milk and yogurt, miso, soy sprouts and green soybeans (*see picture*) every day.

There's a recipe using the beans on page 60.

- Base your meals on whole grains and pulses. Of the grains, well-cooked millet, quinoa, and buckwheat are particularly digestible. Buckwheat is especially beneficial because of its effect on the circulation.

- Use cold-pressed canola oil for cooking, but only over a gentle heat.

- Include daily sources of the omega-3 oils (powdered flaxseeds, flaxseed oil, walnuts, and walnut oil), which the Okinawans get from the fish they eat, as well as from flaxseeds and (small amounts) from tofu. Consider taking an algae-based omega-3 vitamin supplement (see page 12) or eating omega-3 enriched eggs for an extra boost.

- Limit your consumption of alcohol (Okinawan women might have one small drink a day, the men, two), but drink plenty of water, green tea, and jasmine tea.

- Eat as wide a variety of foods, mainly from plant sources, as you can. The Okinawans were found to eat 206 foods over the course of a year, eating 38 different foods regularly and an average of 18 different foods a day.

- Don't eat too much salt.

- Be sure to get enough vitamin D—this is not a problem in the "sunshine states" but in cooler climates elsewhere, take a winter supplement (no more than 10 mcg daily) if in any doubt.

Natural menopause

Okinawan women experience a symptom-free menopause, without the need for drugs and with few complications such as hot flashes or hip fractures. They get estrogens from their diet, mainly from the large amounts of soy they consume. Soybeans contain phytoestrogens, or

plant estrogens, called flavonoids. Other phyto-estrogens are called lignans, and come from flax and other seeds. In fact, all plants, especially pulses, onions, and broccoli, contain some natural estrogens, although not as much as soybeans and flax. The best thing about flavonoids and lignans is that they help protect against any damaging effects of estrogen while retaining all of its benefits.

Foods for longevity

- Turmeric, which has been shown to have numerous healing powers (see page 56).

- Sweet potatoes, which are rich in vitamin A, are sweet and filling, yet won't make your blood sugar rise (unlike ordinary potatoes).

- Kuzu or arrowroot (see page 159).

- Seaweed—kombu, nori, hijiki, wakame (see page 122).

- Blueberries.

- Squash, carrots, zucchini, peppers, onions.

- Sprouted beans (see page 67).

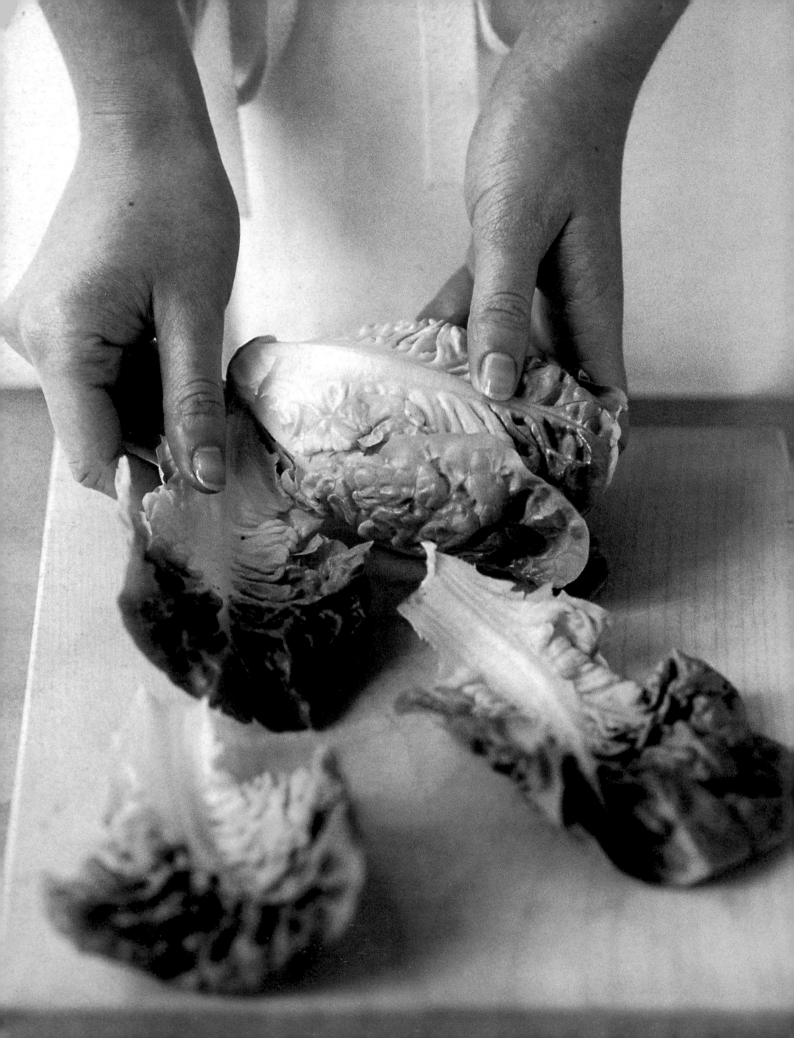

SALADS AND VEGETABLES

ONE OF THE REASONS A VEGETARIAN OR VEGAN DIET IS SO HEALTH GIVING IS BECAUSE IT CONTAINS SO MANY FRESH VEGETABLES, USED IN EVERY WAY POSSIBLE—RAW, COOKED, IN APPETIZERS AND ENTREES, AS SIDE DISHES, AND SO ON. MANY MEALS CONSIST OF NOTHING BUT VEGETABLES, AND THEY'RE SO VARIED, COLORFUL, AND DELICIOUS THAT IT'S NO PROBLEM AT ALL TO EAT THE RECOMMENDED FIVE PORTIONS A DAY. IN FACT, MANY VEGETARIANS EAT AT LEAST DOUBLE THAT AMOUNT. ORGANIC VEGETABLES ARE BEST IF YOU CAN GET THEM, BUT IT'S NOT A PROBLEM IF YOU CAN'T; ANY VEGETABLES ARE FINE.

GREEN PEA SOUP WITH MINT

This is so easy and so good. The simple method is unusual but really effective, and the finishing touch is a swirl of thick yogurt and some fresh mint leaves. It's also delicious when served chilled.

serves 4

2 pound (900-g package) frozen garden peas,
   or fresh peas in the pod if available
1 large onion, roughly chopped
6 garlic cloves
salt and freshly ground black pepper

TO FINISH
3–4 tablespoons thick plain yogurt
fresh mint leaves to garnish

Put the peas into a saucepan with 5 cups (1.2 liters) water, the onion, and garlic. Cover, and simmer for 10–15 minutes, or until the onion and garlic are tender.

Blend in a food processor until puréed, then return to the saucepan. Thin, if necessary, with a little more water and season with salt and freshly ground black pepper. Reheat, then ladle into bowls, top with a swirl of yogurt, a grinding of black pepper, and mint leaves, and serve.

TOMATO AND RED PEPPER SOUP WITH AVOCADO

Tomato soup appeals to all age groups, and this one is particularly
delicious, with the added sweetness of red peppers.

serves 6

4 red bell peppers
1 pound 10 ounces (750 g) tomatoes
1 onion, roughly chopped
2 fat garlic cloves
2½ cups (600 ml) vegetable broth
salt and coarsely ground black pepper
juice of ½ a lemon
1 medium avocado
6 tablespoons dairy cream
6 basil leaves, torn

Halve, seed, and roughly chop the bell peppers, then quarter the tomatoes. Put them into a saucepan
with the onion, garlic cloves, and the broth.

Simmer for 30 minutes or until the peppers are very tender. Purée in a blender or food processor, then
pass the mixture through a sieve into a clean saucepan. Reheat, then season with salt, pepper, and half of
the lemon juice.

Peel, pit, and finely dice the avocado. Place in a bowl, toss in the remaining lemon juice, and season with salt.

Ladle the soup into warmed bowls. Swirl each bowl with a little cream, then top with a tablespoon of
avocado, some torn basil leaves, and a sprinkling of coarsely ground black pepper.

BRAISED VEGETABLES WITH LEMON AND PARSLEY

This is a very useful, not to mention delicious dish, that can be made in advance and reheated—it just goes on getting better. It also tastes good cold if there's any left over. You can use other mixtures of vegetables—quarters of fennel are good—but I like the vibrant colors of this combination.

serves 4

pared rind and juice of 1 lemon
4 tablespoons olive oil
bunch of flat-leaf parsley
2 bay leaves
2 or 3 sprigs of thyme
4 large carrots, cut into sticks
2 red bell peppers, seeded and cut into chunks
2 cups (225 g) broccoli, cut into florets
2 cups (225 g) snow peas, halved lengthwise
bunch of green onions (scallions), trimmed and sliced
salt and freshly ground black pepper

Put the pared lemon rind into a large saucepan with the olive oil, ½ cup (125 ml) water, the stalks of the parsley, bay leaves, and sprigs of thyme.

Bring to the boil, then add the carrots. Simmer for about 5 minutes, to blanch the carrots, then add the peppers, and cook for a further 5 minutes.

Add the broccoli and cook for about 4 minutes, until it is beginning to soften, then add the snow peas and green onions (scallions), and cook for a further 2 minutes or so, until they're just tender.

Add the lemon juice and season with salt and pepper. Just before serving, discard the bay leaves, then chop the parsley leaves and stir them in.

LITTLE GEM, ENDIVE, AND WATERCRESS SALAD

This is a fresh-tasting mixture of contrasting leaves with a thick golden mustard dressing. You can vary the leaves—a package of mixed baby leaves is nice if you can't find watercress.

serves 2–4

2 Little Gem lettuces or romaine hearts
2 heads of Belgian endive
bunch or package of watercress

FOR THE MUSTARD VINAIGRETTE
1 teaspoon Dijon mustard
½ garlic clove, crushed
1 tablespoon red wine vinegar
   or cider vinegar
coarse or kosher salt
3 tablespoons olive oil
freshly ground black pepper

Cut the lettuces into thick wedges—sixths or eighths—right down through their stems. Remove the outer leaves from the Belgian endive, then cut the hearts into quarters or eighths. If you're using a bunch of watercress, remove the thickest part of the stems. Wash all the leaves and shake dry, then heap them up on a serving dish or put them into a salad bowl.

For the vinaigrette, put the mustard, garlic, vinegar, and a little salt into a bowl and mix with a fork or small whisk, then gradually whisk in the oil. Season to taste.

To serve, sprinkle the leaves with the vinaigrette, pour it around the salad, and grind black pepper over the top.

VINAIGRETTE FOR A PARTY I generally mix a dressing as and when I need it, often straight into the salad bowl. However, there are times when it's handy to make up a batch for a party, or to keep a bottle in the refrigerator. To make about 1 scant cup (200 ml), increase the quantities given to 1 tablespoon Dijon or Dijon-style mustard, 1 large garlic clove, 3 tablespoons red wine vinegar or cider vinegar and 9 tablespoons olive oil, with salt and pepper to taste. Simply shake together in a jar or bottle until the mixture emulsifies. This will keep well in the refrigerator for several weeks, just give it a shake before you use it.

MARINATED OLIVES

Wonderful as a snack, simple salad accompaniment, or quick appetizer—
just serve with some good bread—and so pretty. Buy the best unpitted
olives you can find—I like a mixture of Kalamata and green Queen olives.

serves 4

**1 cup (250 g) mixed (unpitted) olives,
    including Kalamata and green Queen or Spanish olives
pared zest of 1 organic orange
1 large garlic clove, thinly sliced
¼ teaspoon dried red chili pepper flakes
½ teaspoon coriander seeds
½ teaspoon fennel seeds
1–2 tablespoons chopped flat-leaf parsley
2 tablespoons freshly squeezed orange juice
2 tablespoons fruity olive oil**

Put the olives into a bowl with all the other ingredients and mix together. Leave for at least 1 hour—
longer if possible—for the flavors to mingle.

SPINACH

For spinach, you don't need any water. Just cram all the leaves into a large saucepan. They'll soon produce their own liquid and can bubble away for 4–8 minutes, or until tender. It helps to push them down into the pan and kind of chop them at the same time with the tip of a metal spatula. Drain well in a colander once they're tender.

MY MOTHER'S WONDERFUL BRUSSELS SPROUTS

I know lots of people hate Brussels sprouts, and I do too, unless they're done my mother's way! Choose tiny, hard ones, trim as necessary and then—and this is the important part—cut them completely in half. Cook them in ½–1 inch (1–2.5 cm) boiling water in a covered pan for no longer than 5–6 minutes, until they're only just tender. Then drain immediately, return to the pan with a large lump of butter or a swirl of oil, and season with salt, freshly ground black pepper, and grated nutmeg, or a dash of celery salt to taste, and tell me they're not wonderful!

PERFECT GREEN VEGETABLES

The secret of cooking vegetables such as cabbage, green beans. and all leaves except spinach, is to use just a little water—½–1 inch (1–2.5 cm) in the bottom of the pan. Bring it to the boil, then add the vegetables—make sure the cabbage is well shredded—and cover with the lid. This means the vegetables half boil, half steam, and most cook in anything from 4 to 8 minutes. Keep testing until they're just right for you, then drain, season with salt and pepper, a swirl of oil or butter if you like, and serve. There's goodness and flavor in the water, so if you know you're going to need vegetable broth, it's worth keeping.

MASHED POTATOES

Although high on the glycemic index—they can be replaced with Millet and Cauliflower Mash (see *page 132*)—mashed potatoes are the ultimate comfort food and there are times when nothing else will do. Peel 1 pound 10 ounces (750 g) potatoes and cut into even-sized chunks. Boil until tender. Drain, then mash with a potato masher or ricer—don't blend in a food processor or you'll end up with glue! Add a large knob of butter or a tablespoon or two of olive oil, salt, pepper, and enough cream or milk to make a light and creamy consistency.

BAKED POTATOES AND BIRCHER POTATOES

Potatoes in their skins are delicious, contain lots of nutrients, and have a fairly low glycemic index. For baked potatoes, choose large potatoes (I like to use organic), scrub, prick, place on a baking sheet, and bake in a hot oven—450°F (230°C)—for 1–1½ hours, depending on the size of the potatoes, until they feel soft when squeezed. Serve at once, while the skins are lovely and crisp.

For Bircher potatoes (named after the Swiss doctor Bircher Benner, who invented muesli), halve the potatoes and rub all over with oil before placing cut-side down on a cookie sheet, and baking as described above. They cook quicker—about 45 minutes—and when they're done the flesh will be tender and the cut surface crisp and golden-brown.

ROAST POTATOES

As with mashed potatoes, there are times when nothing else but the real thing will do. Preheat the oven to 450°F (230°C). Peel 1 pound 10 ounces (750 g) potatoes and cut into even-sized pieces, about 1¼ inch (3 cm) square. Put into a saucepan, cover with water, bring to the boil, cover, and cook for about 8 minutes, or until the potatoes have softened slightly but are still firm. Drain well, then shake the potatoes in the covered pan to roughen the edges so they'll brown better. Meanwhile, pour a thin layer of canola oil (about ⅛ inch/ 3 mm) into a roasting pan and place into the oven to heat. Tip the parboiled potatoes into the fat and turn them quickly so they are coated all over in the oil. Then return them to the oven and bake for 45–60 minutes, or until they're crisp and golden-brown, turning them once or twice so they cook evenly. Serve immediately.

GOLDEN THAI CURRY

This is very easy to make and everyone loves it. Unless you grow your own limes, you can find freeze-dried lime leaves in the spices section of large supermarkets.

serves 4

1 tablespoon sesame oil
1 tablespoon Thai red curry paste
1 red pepper, seeded and cut into ½-inch (1-cm) pieces
1 golden pepper, seeded and cut into ½-inch (1-cm) pieces
4 large green onions (scallions), chopped
1 medium zucchini, cut into ½-inch (1-cm) chunks
4 ounces (115 g) baby corn cobs, halved
4 ounces (115 g) snow peas or sugar snap peas
1 cup (140 g) button mushrooms, washed
1¾ cups (400 ml) canned organic coconut milk
6 lime leaves
½ teaspoon turmeric
2 garlic cloves, crushed
salt and freshly ground black pepper
4 tablespoons fresh coriander (cilantro), chopped

Heat the sesame oil in a large saucepan or wok, then add the curry paste, followed by all the vegetables. Stir-fry for a few seconds, then cover, and leave to cook for about 5 minutes, or until nearly tender.

Add the coconut milk, lime leaves, turmeric, garlic, and salt and pepper to taste. Stir, then sprinkle with chopped coriander, and serve with hot cooked basmati rice.

COCONUT MILK AND OIL There's increasing evidence of the health benefits of the oil found naturally in coconuts. It's saturated with a high proportion of "good" fat—mostly medium-chain fatty acids—which the body can use efficiently and convert into energy rather than store as fat. Some people report that using coconut butter, creamed coconut, and coconut milk for cooking has helped them lose weight, an effect supported by studies on animals. It also has a positive effect on heart health. Countries such as Sri Lanka, where coconut oil is the main source of dietary fat, have very low rates of heart disease. You can find organic creamed coconut and coconut milk in large supermarkets, and coconut butter is available from good health food stores.

QUICK BROILED MEDITERRANEAN VEGETABLES

This is probably the fast meal that I fall back on most. Get your vegetables under the broiler, then cook grains or pasta to serve with them. Make a batch of Light and Creamy Hummus (*see page 96*) or a pan of Lentil Dal (*see page 105*) and you've got a meal in moments. I like to baste the vegetables in a mixture of lemon juice and olive oil (the peppers don't need basting) to keep them light. For a picture of this dish, turn to page 2.

serves 2–4

1–2 zucchini, halved or quartered lengthwise and cut into 2-inch (5-cm) lengths
I red onion, peeled and cut into sixths
I eggplant, cut into chunks
I tablespoon olive oil
salt
I tablespoon fresh lemon juice
I red and I yellow bell pepper, halved and seeded, then cut into strips
12 black olives, pitted (optional)
several sprigs of basil (optional), torn
freshly ground black pepper

I heat the broiler to high. Put the zucchini, onion, and eggplant chunks onto a metal sheet that will fit under your broiler, brush with the olive oil, lemon juice, and sprinkle with a little salt. Place the sheet under the broiler and cook the vegetables, moving and turning them so that all are evenly coated and cook evenly. I use my hands for this. Then add the bell pepper pieces—these don't need oiling.

Broil for around 20 minutes, or until the vegetables are tender and browned in places, turning after 10 minutes. Stir in black olives and sprinkle with basil and pepper. Serve with grains or pasta and some hummus or dal. If there are any vegetables left over, which hardly ever happens, they're great cold, too.

VARIATIONS Of course, you can vary the vegetables. Sometimes I use just red bell peppers or mix them with olives, which makes a nice appetizer. Zucchini or eggplant, on their own, are also good, with chopped fresh mint mixed in at the end.

MUSHROOM PÂTÉ EN CROÛTE

A pâté or terrine of mushrooms and nuts wrapped in puff pastry has long been a favorite dish of mine. I keep changing and improving it, and this is the best ever. It owes some of its inspiration, especially the brilliant idea of the tarragon, to Nadine Abensur and her Mushroom Wellington. It makes a stunning entrée for a special meal and goes with all the classic sauces, such as Cranberry Sauce (see page 147), horseradish sauce, or a light, tasty Madeira Gravy (see page 146). It slices well and is also great cold.

serves 8

2 large onions, minced
2 tablespoons olive oil
2 garlic cloves, minced
2 cups (250 g) Portobello mushrooms, roughly sliced
1 cup (225 g) cashew nuts, ground in a food processor or coffee grinder
1 cup (225 g) ground almonds
2 cups (225 g) soft whole wheat bread crumbs
2 tablespoons soy sauce
2 tablespoons lemon juice
2 teaspoons dried tarragon
1 teaspoon yeast extract
salt and freshly ground black pepper
1 pound 2 ounces (500 g) puff pastry dough
beaten egg or soy milk, for brushing

Preheat the oven to 400°F (200°C).

In a large saucepan, sauté the onions in the olive oil for 7 minutes, until tender. Add the garlic and mushrooms and cook for a further 5 minutes, or until the mushrooms are tender. Then tip the mixture into a food processor and blend to a purée.

Put the ground cashew nuts and almonds into a bowl with the bread crumbs, mushroom purée, soy sauce, lemon juice, tarragon, and yeast extract, and mix well. The mixture will be quite stiff. Season well with salt and freshly ground black pepper.

Roll the puff pastry dough out on a lightly floured board to make a square about 15 inches (38 cm) in size. Transfer the dough to a cookie sheet and heap the mushroom mixture in the center, shaping it into a loaf.

Make diagonal cuts in the pastry about ½ inch (1 cm) apart, on each side of the mushroom mixture, then fold these up over the mushroom pâté into a sort of braided effect. Tuck in the ends neatly, trim off any extra bits, and brush with beaten egg or soy milk.

Bake 40 minutes, or until the pastry is puffed and golden brown.

CUMIN-ROASTED SWEET POTATOES

Sweet potatoes cook much more quickly than you'd think. You can broil them or grill them on a barbecue and they always turn out well. I love them, children love them. They have more flavor than ordinary potatoes and a lower GI rating. The best are the orange-fleshed kind, that are also called yams.

serves 4

2 pounds 4 ounces (1 kg) sweet potatoes, scrubbed
2 garlic cloves
salt
2 tablespoons ground cumin
2 tablespoons olive oil
2 tablespoons fresh lemon juice
freshly ground black pepper
steak seasoning (variation)

Heat the broiler to high. Cut the sweet potatoes into walnut-sized chunks and arrange on a cookie sheet that will fit under your broiler.

Chop or grate the garlic, then mix with a large pinch of salt and pound to a paste with the tip of your knife. Mix this paste with the cumin, olive oil, lemon juice, and a little pepper, then mix it with the sweet potatoes so that they are coated evenly—I use my hands for this.

Broil for about 10–15 minutes, moving the potatoes around after about 5 minutes so they brown evenly. They're done when you can easily get a knife point into one and they're tinged brown.

An easy variation is to coat the sweet potatoes with just the olive oil and lemon juice, then sprinkle with a dash of steak seasoning, which you can get at any supermarket, before broiling.

TUMBET

A friend of mine told me about this Spanish dish, which she ate in Majorca. It's a wonderful feast of vegetables that you can quickly assemble, then put into the oven and forget, while they cook to a delectable melting tenderness. If there's any left over, it's excellent cold.

serves 4

2 large onions, cut into chunks
1 large eggplant, cut into chunks
3 potatoes, scrubbed and cut into chunks
2 red peppers, seeded and cut into chunks
3 zucchini, cut into chunks
1 head of garlic, cloves peeled and left whole
bunch of flat-leaf parsley, chopped
salt and freshly ground black pepper
6–7 tablespoons olive oil
2 cups (425 g) canned chopped tomatoes

Put all the raw vegetables, the garlic, and parsley into a large shallow oven dish, mixing them together and smoothing them into a flat layer.

Sprinkle with salt and pepper, then pour the oil over them and top with the tomatoes. Season again lightly with salt and pepper.

Bake uncovered at 325°F (160°C) for 2–3 hours, or until the vegetables are tender.

Use sweet potatoes instead of ordinary potatoes for a deliciously sweet mixture with a lower GI rating.

CHUNKY OVEN-BAKED RATATOUILLE

This is a substantial French vegetable mixture, which you can make even more filling, if you wish, by adding a can of drained navy or kidney beans 10 minutes before it's finished cooking and serving with cooked millet or buckwheat. You could cut the vegetables into smaller pieces, in which case they'll cook more quickly, so keep an eye on them.

serves 4

1 large red onion, cut into chunks
1 large zucchini, cut into chunks
1 large eggplant, cut into chunks
2 red and 2 yellow bell peppers,
   seeded and cut into chunks
1 pound (450 g) small tomatoes
   or large cherry tomatoes
4 garlic cloves, chopped
3 tablespoons olive oil
salt and freshly ground black pepper
several sprigs of fresh basil

Preheat the oven to 475°F (240°C).

Put all the vegetables and the garlic in a roasting pan or large, shallow ovenproof dish. Sprinkle with the oil and some salt and pepper, then mix with your hands so that all are coated evenly. Put the dish into the oven and cook, uncovered, for 30–40 minutes, until the vegetables are browned at the edges, tender, and smelling fragrant. Tear the basil leaves over the top and serve.

SPICY RATATOUILLE For a spicy version, stir 1–2 teaspoons cumin seeds and/or 1–2 teaspoons of crushed coriander seeds into the vegetables, and omit the basil.

JUICY RATATOUILLE For a particularly juicy version, use a 1-pound can (425 g) of tomatoes in juice (organic, if possible) instead of the fresh tomatoes, adding them about 20 minutes before the end of the cooking time.

RED ONION AND GOAT CHEESE FLAN

I make this in a 12-inch (30-cm) shallow, fluted tart pan, about ½ inch
(1 cm) deep, with a removable base. To serve it, I transfer it to one of
those large, round ovenproof pizza bakestones that you can buy at any
kitchenware store. It isn't the fastest recipe to make, but you can do it in
stages, and it's so unfailingly popular that it's worth the trouble.

serves 6

FOR THE FILLING
2¼ pounds (1 kg) red onions, thinly sliced
2 tablespoons olive oil
2 tablespoons sugar
3 tablespoons sherry (any type) or red wine
2 tablespoons red wine vinegar
salt and freshly ground black pepper
12 ounces (350 g) firm goat cheese log

FOR THE OLIVE OIL DOUGH
2 cups (225 g) whole wheat pastry flour (see page 188)
½ teaspoon salt
6 tablespoons olive oil

Preheat the oven to 350°F (180°C).

For the filling, cook the onions in the oil in a large saucepan, covered, for about 15 minutes until tender,
stirring every 5 minutes. They must be really soft before you proceed to the next stage.

Add the sugar, sherry or wine, and the vinegar. Then let the mixture simmer gently, uncovered, for about
30 minutes until you have a thick, sticky mixture with hardly any liquid left. Remove from the heat, season
to taste with salt and pepper, and leave to cool.

While the onions are cooking, make the dough. Put the flour and salt into a bowl and carefully measure
in the olive oil and 3 tablespoons of water. Mix to a soft dough, then press evenly into the base and up
the sides of the pie pan to coat it thinly. Bake for 10 minutes, or until crisp.

Spread the onion mixture evenly over the base of the flan. Cut the goat cheese into thin slices and place
on top of the onions, to cover them. Return the flan to the oven and cook for 20–30 minutes, or until
the cheese has melted and browned.

For a vegan variation, use 9 ounces (250 g) grated white vegan cheese instead of the goat cheese.

ROASTED VEGETABLE AND GOAT CHEESE TORTE

This is a lovely dish for a party—a real centerpiece—but it has to be made the night before. A jug of Vinaigrette for a Party (*see page 33*)—make double the quantity—and a leafy green salad go well with the torte.

serves 8

5 red bell peppers, halved and seeded
4 tablespoons balsamic vinegar
salt and freshly ground black pepper
5 eggplant, cut into ¼-inch (6-mm) slices
3 tablespoons olive oil
1 pound 10 ounces (750 g) goat cheese logs (with soft rind), sliced
12 sun-dried tomatoes, chopped
bunch or package of basil

Set the broiler to high. Arrange the peppers on the broiler pan, cut-side down—no need to oil them—and broil for about 10–15 minutes, or until they are really tender and blackened in places. Remove from under the broiler, sprinkle with half the balsamic vinegar and some salt and pepper, and leave to cool.

Brush the eggplant slices on both sides with olive oil. Broil until golden brown on one side, then turn over and broil the other side—they take about 10–15 minutes. Make sure they're really tender. Mix with salt, pepper, and the rest of the balsamic vinegar.

Put a circle of nonstick baking paper into the base of a 9-inch (23-cm) round cake pan with a removable base. Cover the base and sides of the pan with slices of eggplant. Next add a layer of peppers, squashing the halves flat, then top with a layer of goat cheese, half the sun-dried tomatoes, and a thin layer of basil leaves. Repeat the layers, finishing with a layer of eggplant. Put several layers of paper towels on top of the torte and top with a plate. Stand the pan on another plate in case it oozes liquid, then put a weight on it, and leave for several hours, or overnight, in a cool place.

To serve, remove the paper towels from the top of the torte and blot with some clean paper towels, if necessary. Invert the torte onto a plate—it should slip out easily—blot again as necessary and sprinkle with some more basil leaves.

ROASTED VEGETABLE AND AVOCADO TORTE For a vegan variation, instead of the goat cheese, use 4 large, ripe avocados, peeled, pitted, sliced, and tossed in lemon juice, salt, and pepper, and layer with the vegetables as described above.

MUSHROOM AND CHESTNUT TART

I'm really pleased with the pastry dough I'm using here, which I invented to provide both protein for the dish and a change from wheat-based dough. It's easy to make and turns out crisp and delicious, contrasting with the creamy filling. The chestnuts give it a Christmas feel and you can emphasize this, if you like, by garnishing the tart with some sprigs of fresh rosemary and a few cranberries. I use the same pan and serving platter for this tart as for the Red Onion and Goat Cheese Flan (see page 47).

serves 6

FOR THE ALMOND AND ROSEMARY PASTRY DOUGH
olive oil, for greasing
7 ounces (200 g) onion, roughly chopped
4 garlic cloves
3½ cups (400 g) ground almonds
I teaspoon dried rosemary
salt and freshly ground black pepper

FOR THE FILLING
2 tablespoons olive oil
8 cups (900 g) Portobello mushrooms, sliced
4 garlic cloves, chopped or crushed
2 tablespoons arrowroot (see page 159)
I cup (250 ml) light cream or soy milk
7-ounce (200-g) vacuum pack whole chestnuts
juice of ½ a lemon
salt and freshly ground black pepper
sprigs of rosemary and fresh cranberries, to garnish (optional)

Preheat the oven to 350°F (180°C). Lightly brush a shallow, loose-bottomed pie pan with olive oil.

Start by making the dough. Put the onion and garlic into a food processor and process until finely chopped. Add the ground almonds, rosemary, and some salt and pepper and process again, until the mixture forms into a dough. Press this evenly into the base and up the sides of the pie pan. Bake for 15 minutes or until golden brown.

Meanwhile, make the filling. Heat the oil in a saucepan, add the mushrooms and cook, uncovered, for about 5 minutes or until tender. Stir in the garlic and arrowroot, then add the cream and stir gently over the heat until thickened. Add the chestnuts, lemon juice, salt and freshly ground black pepper.

It's best to fill the tart just before serving. Make sure both the pastry shell and filling are hot, then spoon the filling evenly into the shell. Garnish with sprigs of fresh rosemary and cranberries, if you wish.

GRATIN DAUPHINOISE WITH WILD MUSHROOMS

Although made from simple ingredients, this dish is so rich and wonderful
that it makes a great dish for entertaining. Serve with the Little Gem,
Belgian Endive, and Watercress Salad (see *page 33*).

serves 6

4 tablespoons (50 g) butter
1 pound 2 ounces (500 g) wild mushrooms,
**   cleaned and sliced**
4½ pounds (2 kg) potatoes
6 garlic cloves, crushed
salt and freshly ground black pepepper
freshly grated nutmeg
1¼ cups (300 ml) heavy cream
3 tablespoons truffle oil

Preheat the oven to 350°F (180°C).

Heat three-quarters of the butter in a saucepan, add the mushrooms, and cook for 5–10 minutes, or
until the mushrooms are tender. If there's any liquid, strain it off and save it.

Slice the potatoes—which can be peeled or not, as you wish—as thinly as you can; a food processor
with a slicing attachment is great for this. Put the potato slices into a colander and rinse under cold
running water to get rid of the excess starch.

Peel and chop the garlic and mix with the remaining butter. Use this mixture to grease a large shallow
ovenproof dish generously. I use one that measures 9½ × 12 inches (24 × 30 cm).

Layer half the potatoes into the dish and season well with salt, pepper, and nutmeg. Spoon the
mushrooms on top, season again, then top with the remaining potatoes, and season once more.

Pour the cream over the top, then fill the cream carton with any liquid that you strained from the
mushrooms, plus water to fill it to the top, and pour that over the potatoes, too.

Drizzle the truffle oil over the top and bake for 1½ hours, or until you can easily insert a sharp knife into
the potatoes and the top is golden brown. Part of the joy of this dish is the contrast between the
crunchy top and the meltingly tender potato underneath. If the top seems to be browning too quickly,
cover it with aluminum foil, but remove the foil 10–15 minutes before the end of the cooking time, to
crisp the top.

You can make a vegan version of this dish using 2½ cups (600 ml) of vegetable broth instead of the
cream and water.

QUICK AFTER WORK MEALS

Pasta with Watercress Pesto (*see page 68*)
Tomato and Avocado Salad (*see Fresh Tomato and Coriander Chutney, page 66*)
Oranges and Passion Fruit (*see page 165*)

Best-ever Chili (*see page 99*)
Baked potato or fluffy cooked millet
Avocado Dip with Chopped Tomato and Coriander (*see page 87*)
Fresh fruits

Spinach Curry (*see page 56*)
Lentil Dal (*see page 105*)
Brown basmati rice
Fresh Tomato and Coriander Chutney (*see page 66*)
Exotic Fruit Compote (*see page 172*)

Golden Thai Curry (see *page 38*)
Grilled Spiced Tofu with Peppers (see *page 148*)
Lychees, Kiwis, and Ginger (see *page 166*)

Quick Broiled Mediterranean Vegetables (see *page 39*)
Light and Creamy Hummus (see *page 86*) or Mediterranean Bean Pâté (see *page 87*)
Buckwheat with Lemon and Herbs (see *page 130*) or fluffy cooked quinoa

Spaghetti with Red Hot Sauce (see *page 63*)
Green salad
Peach and Blueberry Compote (see *page 175*)

KERALAN CURRY

It's a wonderful dish for a party—everyone loves it, and you can make it a day in advance. Serve with Lemon Rice (*see page 137*), Fresh Tomato and Coriander Chutney (*see page 66*), mango chutney, and some warm poppadoms. If there's any curry left over it freezes very well.

serves 6

1 tablespoon oil
2 onions, minced
4 carrots, sliced
1 baking potato, cut into ½-inch (1-cm) cubes
1 small cauliflower, divided into small florets
1½ cups (250 g) green beans, trimmed and halved
1 green chili pepper, seeded and chopped
1½ teaspoons ground coriander
1½ teaspoons ground cumin
1½ teaspoons ground turmeric
1¾ cups (400 ml) coconut milk

FOR THE CURRY PASTE
1 beefsteak tomato, skinned and chopped
6 garlic cloves, crushed
3 × 1-inch (2.5-cm) pieces fresh ginger, peeled and roughly chopped
1½ teaspoons fennel seeds
6 cloves
6 cardamom pods
salt

Heat the oil in a large saucepan, add the onion, and sauté for 5 minutes. Then stir in the carrots, cover the pan, reduce the heat to low, and cook for 10 minutes. Add the potato, cover, and cook gently for another 10 minutes, before adding the cauliflower, beans, and chili. Stir, cover, and cook gently until all the vegetables are nearly tender, then stir in the coriander, cumin, and turmeric and cook for another minute or two longer.

While the vegetables are cooking, make the curry paste. Put all the ingredients into a food processor and blend to a purée.

Add the curry paste to the vegetables, stirring well. Cook for 5–10 minutes, then pour in the coconut milk and season with salt to taste (approximately 1 teaspoon). Cook for a further minute or two until the coconut milk is hot. Serve immediately.

SPINACH CURRY (SAG BHAJI)

Iron-rich, slightly bitter, dark green spinach leaves, cooked with warming spices, make a wonderful side dish for curries. I love them with boiled or steamed brown basmati rice, a few tablespoons of Lentil Dal (*see page 105*) and some sliced tomatoes.

serves 2–4

1 onion, chopped
1 tablespoon canola oil
2 garlic cloves, crushed
1 tablespoon fresh ginger, grated
1 teaspoon turmeric
1 teaspoon ground coriander
4 cups (500 g) spinach leaves
salt and freshly ground black pepper

Sauté the onion in the oil in a large pan for 10 minutes, covered, until the onion is tender.

Add the garlic, ginger, turmeric, and coriander. Stir for a few seconds over the heat, until you can smell the fragrance, then add the spinach and stir it around to coat it with the spices.

Cover, then cook over a moderate heat for about 10 minutes, until the spinach is soft and much reduced in volume, stirring from time to time. Season with salt and pepper and serve.

THE MAGIC OF TURMERIC Turmeric, a staple ingredient in Eastern cookery that gives curries their golden color, has been found to have remarkable therapeutic properties. Clinical studies have shown that not only does it help prevent the formation of tumors in the body, giving protection from cancer, it also lowers cholesterol levels, helps to keep the blood thin, increases bile production and flow, and exerts a powerful anti-inflammatory action, which protects the stomach and eases irritable bowel syndrome. A pinch of turmeric a day really could keep the doctor away.

CABBAGE THORAN

This makes a very pleasant side dish for a selection of curries, or you can serve it as I usually do, with some steamed or boiled brown basmati rice and Lentil Dal (*see page 105*). Children like it because of the coconut, so it's a good way of getting them to eat their greens.

serves 2–4

  1 onion, sliced
  1 tablespoon canola oil
  1 teaspoon mustard seeds
  1/2 teaspoon turmeric
  1/2 cinnamon stick, broken
  12 curry leaves or 1/2 teaspoon curry powder
  1 cup (225 g) shredded cabbage
  3 tablespoons (50 g) unsweetened shredded coconut
  salt and freshly ground black pepper

Cook the onion in the oil in a covered pan for about 7 minutes, until it is almost tender.

Add the mustard seeds, turmeric, cinnamon stick, and curry leaves or powder. Stir for a few seconds, until they smell fragrant, then add the cabbage and coconut.

Stir well, then cover, and leave to cook gently for about 10 minutes, or until the cabbage is tender. Season with salt and pepper and serve.

TIME-SAVING WITH INDIAN MEALS A meal consisting of a lot of different spicy dishes is a delight, but who has the time to make them all? One way of doing it is to make more than you need each time and save what's left. Curries keep very well for several days in the refrigerator and continue to improve as the flavors blend. So by adding a new dish every day to serve with the others, you get a constantly evolving selection without much effort.

PASTA AND NOODLES

WE ALL KNOW AND LOVE WHEAT PASTAS SUCH AS SPAGHETTI, BUT I WOULD ALSO URGE YOU TO TRY SOME OF THE MORE UNUSUAL PASTAS, FOR DIFFERENT FLAVORS AND HEALTH BENEFITS. TRY WHOLE WHEAT PASTA, FOR INSTANCE, WHICH HAS IMPROVED GREATLY OVER THE YEARS; BUCKWHEAT PASTA OR TRADITIONAL SOBA (BUCKWHEAT) NOODLES FROM JAPAN; AND TRANSPARENT MUNG BEAN NOODLES AND SOY PASTA THAT CONTRIBUTE EXTRA PROTEIN TO A VEGETARIAN MEAL IN ADDITION TO TASTING GOOD.

SOBA WITH GREEN SOYBEANS

Cold noodles may sound strange at first, but they are very popular in Japan, and once you try them like this they're quite addictive. I love them with a side dish of green soybeans, or *edamame* as they're known in Japan (*see picture on page 25*). You can buy them frozen from oriental grocery stores. Try them if you can find them—suck the beans out of the pods into your mouth and discard the pods—but if you can't, the noodles are still very good on their own.

serves 2

> 9 ounces (250 g) soba (buckwheat noodles)
> 1 package frozen green soybeans (*edamame*)
> 4 teaspoons sesame seeds
> 1 tablespoon toasted sesame oil
> 1 tablespoon mirin, apple juice concentrate,
>   or clear honey
> 1 tablespoon rice vinegar
> 1 tablespoon soy sauce
> 4 green onions (scallions), shredded

Bring two saucepans of water to the boil, a big one for the noodles and another for the soybeans. Cook the noodles for around 4 minutes, or according to the directions on the package. Add a pinch of salt to the soybean water, and cook the soybeans for about the same amount of time, or until they are tender (you probably won't understand the package directions unless you can read Japanese).

Meanwhile, toast the sesame seeds by stirring them in a small, dry saucepan for a minute or two until they smell toasted and start to jump around in the pan. Remove from the heat and pour them onto a plate so they don't continue cooking and become burned and bitter.

Drain the noodles in a colander and rinse under cold running water. Put them in a bowl, then add the sesame oil, mirin, apple juice concentrate or honey, the vinegar, and soy sauce. Toss the noodles so they are evenly coated, then stir in the shredded green onions and toasted sesame seeds. Drain the soybeans and transfer to a bowl. Serve with the noodles.

NOODLES WITH PEANUT AND GINGER SAUCE

In this recipe, with its oriental overtones, peanut butter is flavored and then used to coat the pasta, rather like pesto. It's delicious made with soba (buckwheat noodles), but also works well with other kinds of pasta, especially spaghetti. You can make this using almond or hazelnut butter, both of which you can find at good health food stores, in place of the peanut butter.

serves 2

9 ounces (250 g) soba (buckwheat noodles)
2 tablespoons peanut butter, crunchy or smooth
  (ideally an organic variety not containing palm oil)
2 tablespoons soy sauce
1 tablespoon mirin (*see below*), rice syrup, or honey
1 tablespoon grated fresh ginger
2 garlic cloves, crushed
1 tablespoon toasted sesame oil
a few red chili pepper flakes
a little fresh coriander (cilantro), chopped

Bring a large saucepan of water to the boil and cook the soba for around 4 minutes, or according to the directions on the package.

Meanwhile, make the dressing by mixing the peanut butter with the soy sauce, mirin, rice syrup or honey, the ginger, and garlic.

When the noodles are done, drain them in a colander and return them to the pan. Swirl in the sesame oil, then add the peanut mixture and toss the noodles so that they are well coated.

Sprinkle with a few chili pepper flakes, then serve, scattered with some chopped coriander.

MIRIN is a natural sweetener used in Japanese cooking, made from sweet rice fermented in spring water. You can buy it from specialty health food shops and some big supermarkets. Make sure you buy a naturally fermented product, rather than one containing sugar.

SPAGHETTI WITH RED HOT SAUCE

This sauce is a brilliant scarlet, as warming to look at as it is to eat, with the sweetness of the bell pepper and the kick of the chili.

serves 2

2 tablespoons olive oil
1 onion, minced
1 red bell pepper, diced
2 scant cups (425 g) canned tomatoes in juice
1 garlic clove, minced
1/2 teaspoon dried red chili pepper flakes
salt and freshly ground black pepper
9 ounces (250 g) spaghetti
Parmesan cheese, flaked or grated, to serve (optional)

For the sauce, heat 1 tablespoon of the oil in a saucepan, add the onion, cover, and cook gently for 5 minutes. Then add the red bell pepper and cook for another 5 minutes. Pour in the tomatoes, chopping them a little with the spoon. Add the garlic and chili pepper flakes, stir, and leave to cook, uncovered, for around 15 minutes, or until thick. Season with salt and pepper.

Meanwhile, bring a big saucepan of water to the boil for the spaghetti. Add the spaghetti and cook according to the package directions, but bite a piece a minute or so before the package says it will be ready to make sure it will really be al dente. Drain the pasta and put it back into the still-warm pot.

If you're going to serve the sauce mixed with the pasta, add it now and season to taste (you don't need the rest of the oil). Alternatively, if you'd rather serve the sauce sitting on top of the pasta, swirl the pasta with the rest of the oil and some seasoning, then serve it, and spoon the sauce on top. Serve the cheese separately, if using.

NOODLES WITH STIR-FRIED VEGETABLES

The best noodles for this dish are Chinese cellophane noodles made from mung beans, but this stir-fried mixture will work with any long, thin pasta, even spaghetti. And if you're really pressed for time, try using a package of frozen stir-fry vegetables instead of fresh ones.

serves 2

9 ounces (250 g) cellophane noodles
1 tablespoon toasted sesame oil
⅔ cup (140 g) baby corncobs, halved diagonally
⅔ cup (140 g) snow peas, split vertically into shreds
4 green onions (scallions), sliced
1 large red chili pepper, seeded and sliced
1 carrot, sliced into thin shreds
1 cup (225 g) canned water chestnuts, drained
soy sauce
salt and pepper to taste
2 tablespoons fresh coriander (cilantro), chopped

Prepare the noodles according to the directions on the package. If they are cellophane noodles, this usually means putting them into a bowl, covering with boiling water, and leaving to stand for 5 minutes.

Meanwhile, heat the oil in a large saucepan and add the corn, snow peas, green onions, chili, carrot, and water chestnuts. Stir-fry for about 3 minutes, until the vegetables are heated through but still crunchy.

Season with a few drops of soy sauce and salt and pepper to taste. Stir in the chopped coriander and serve.

TOFU MAYONNAISE

I love this dressing because it has the creaminess of traditional mayonnaise with only a tiny fraction of the calories, plus all the goodness and protein of tofu. A big spoonful turns a salad into a light entrée. Drain a 9-ounce (250-g) block of tofu, break it up roughly, and put it in a food processor with a crushed garlic clove, 1 teaspoon Dijon mustard, and the juice of half a lemon, and blend to a thick, creamy consistency. If you want it thinner, you can add a little water or soy milk. Season with salt and freshly ground black pepper.

FRESH TOMATO AND CORIANDER CHUTNEY

This is what I love to serve with Indian curries and spicy foods. All you do is cut up 1 cup (225 g) fresh tomatoes, season with salt and pepper, and mix with a tablespoon of chopped fresh coriander (cilantro). Sometimes I squeeze a little lemon juice into the mixture or add a tablespoon of thinly sliced green onion (scallion) or a white or yellow onion. You can vary the herbs: fresh basil or mint is nice instead of the coriander. As an alternative, add a large, peeled, pitted, and chopped avocado to the tomatoes, and use basil instead of coriander. Season with salt and pepper and add a squeeze of lemon juice.

MIDDLE EASTERN CARROT SALAD

A pile of freshly grated carrot is often included in Middle Eastern salad platters, and looks and tastes so vibrant that I can eat it just as it is. If it's juicy, and quite finely grated, I don't think it needs much dressing—a dash of vinaigrette maybe, or some Asian Dressing (*see opposite*), or simply a squeeze of orange or lemon juice. You can add chopped fresh herbs—parsley, mint, or chives—or some poppyseeds, sesame seeds, sunflower seeds or pumpkin seeds (pepitas), which you could stir in a pan over the heat for a minute or two until they start to "pop" and smell wonderful. Some people like to stir in raisins, too.

ASIAN DRESSING

You can make a delicious, completely fat-free dressing, using equal parts of a good soy sauce, lime juice, and rice vinegar. Mix together and use like a vinaigrette. You could use lemon juice but the lime juice gives it extra fragrance; and you could sweeten it a little with a dash of mirin or apple juice concentrate, if you wish.

RAITA

This is really just thick yogurt with herbs or vegetables added. Don't make it too far in advance or it may go watery. Simply stir 2 tablespoons of chopped fresh coriander (cilantro), mint, or chives into 1¼ cups (300 ml) yogurt, or use half a peeled and diced cucumber (blotted on paper towels to remove some of the moisture), 1–2 shredded green onions (scallions), or a coarsely grated carrot.

SPROUTED BEANS AND SEEDS

You can buy the beans ready sprouted, but they are also easy to make yourself. Just soak overnight a couple of tablespoons of your chosen beans or seeds overnight—chickpeas, green lentils, mung beans, alfalfa seeds, or sunflower seeds—or you can buy packages of sprouting mix at some health food stores. Next day, rinse them and put them into a jar with a piece of cheesecloth secured over the top with an elastic band, or use a special bean-sprouting jar with a perforated lid. Rinse twice a day by filling the jar with water through the cheesecloth/lid, shaking it around and draining it. Keep the jar on its side, preferably in a dark place or covered with a cloth, while the beans or seeds germinate. The sprouts will appear in a couple of days and you can eat them in 3–4 days. Rinse first, then add to salads.

PASTA WITH WATERCRESS PESTO

Watercress pesto is brilliant green with a very perky flavor. If you've got a food processor you can blend it up in a jiffy and it seems to go with almost any shape of pasta. To toast the pine nuts, spread them out on a dry cookie sheet and put under a hot broiler for a minute or so. As soon as they turn golden, remove them from under the broiler, and tip them into a cold dish so they don't continue cooking and burn.

serves 2

9 ounces (250 g) pasta, such as penne or spaghetti
1 large garlic clove, peeled
2 tablespoons (25 g) pine nuts, lightly toasted
2 tablespoons (25 g) fresh Parmesan cheese, cut into small pieces,
  plus extra, grated, to serve (optional)
3½ ounces (90-g package or bunch) watercress, stems removed
2 tablespoons olive oil
salt and freshly ground black pepper

Cook the pasta in a big saucepan of boiling water according to the package directions. Try a piece a minute or so before the package says it will be ready to make sure you get it really al dente.

Meanwhile, make the pesto. Put all the remaining ingredients into a food processor and blend to a bright green paste, with no visible chunks of cheese or nut showing. You may need to scrape down the sides and blend again a couple of times to achieve this. Season with salt and pepper.

When the pasta is done, drain it in a colander then tip it back into the still-warm saucepan. Add the pesto, swirl it around so all the pasta is coated, then serve with the extra Parmesan, if using.

For a vegan alternative, leave out the Parmesan cheese and instead use double the amount of pine nuts. If this pesto is a little stiff, stir in a tablespoon of the pasta cooking water to loosen it before mixing it with the pasta.

LINGUINE WITH PEPPERS, BASIL, AND PECORINO

This is blissfully easy to make and very popular. You could include a few black olives as well, for piquancy.

serves 2

1 red bell pepper, halved and seeded
1 yellow bell pepper, halved and seeded
9 ounces (250 g) linguine or other pasta
1 tablespoon olive oil
1 garlic clove, crushed
salt and freshly ground black pepper
3 or 4 sprigs of basil, torn
Pecorino cheese, flaked or grated, to serve

Preheat the broiler. Put the peppers, cut-side downward, on a broiler pan and broil until the skin is blistered and blackened in places. Remove from the broiler and leave until cool enough to handle, then strip off the skin (if you wish) and slice the peppers into strips.

Meanwhile, bring a big saucepan of water to the boil and add the pasta. Cook according to the package directions, but bite a piece a minute or so before the package says it will be ready, to make sure you get it really al dente.

Drain the pasta in a colander, then return it to the still-warm saucepan with the olive oil, garlic, and salt and pepper to taste. Swirl it around, stir in the bell pepper strips and basil, then serve. Hand around the cheese separately.

For a vegan alternative, make exactly as described but serve without the cheese; an extra tablespoon of good olive oil, added at the table, is a nice touch.

VEGETARIAN AND VEGAN CHEESES Many cheeses are now made with vegetarian rennet (instead of rennet made from animals' digestive juices), and these are usually labeled as such. However, some vegetarian cheeses do not advertise the fact, so it's always worth asking. There is a vegetarian Parmesan, but if you like a good, strong flavor, you might prefer to use a traditionally made hard Pecorino, which is vegetarian. Vegan cheeses have improved enormously and can often be used instead of dairy cheese.

PASTA WITH CHERRY TOMATOES AND ASPARAGUS

This is such an easy pasta dish. The "sauce" makes itself under the broiler while you cook the pasta. It's low in fat—and could be completely fat-free if you like.

serves 2

1¼ cups (300 g) cherry tomatoes, stems removed
6 ounces (175 g) asparagus tips
2 tablespoons olive oil
8 ounces (225 g) pasta (I like to use fettuccini)
salt and freshly ground black pepper
few sprigs of basil

Put a big saucepan of water on the stove to heat for the pasta. Set the broiler to high.

Place the cherry tomatoes in a single layer in a broiler pan. Brush the asparagus tips with half the olive oil, then cut the spears in half and put these in the broiler pan, too. Place under the hot broiler.

When the water comes to a rolling boil, add the pasta and cook for about 12 minutes, or according to the directions on the package, but bite a piece a minute or so before the package says it will be ready to make sure you get it really al dente. Drain in a colander, then return to the pan with the rest of the olive oil and season to taste.

While the pasta is cooking, keep an eye on the asparagus and tomatoes; the tomatoes need to be on the point of collapse and the asparagus should be just tender to the point of a knife and perhaps tinged brown in places. Add the tomatoes and asparagus to the pasta. Tear some basil leaves and sprinkle them over the dish before serving.

For a fat-free version, broil the tomatoes as described (without oil) but don't broil the asparagus; just throw this in with the pasta a couple of minutes before the pasta is cooked. Drain them together and then stir in the seasoning, tomatoes, and basil as before.

For the pasta, you could also use wheat-free, soy, parsley, and garlic pasta twists (see *page 188*).

FUSILLI WITH UNCOOKED TOMATO AND BASIL SAUCE

I never tire of this classic, summer pasta dish. Made with fragrant sun-ripened tomatoes and basil; pale green, unfiltered, cold-pressed olive oil; and some buttery chunks of avocado, it's a delight and takes virtually no time to prepare. It's delicious made with fusilli, but for a change I also use buckwheat pasta twists and the protein-rich, wheat-free soy parsley and garlic pasta twists you can find at specialty health food stores (*see page 188*), which I love to eat as long as they're really al dente (they take six minutes to cook—much less time than the package says).

serves 2–3

9 ounces (250 g) fusilli
2 cups (450 g) chopped tomatoes
2 garlic cloves, crushed or minced
2 good sprigs of fresh basil, leaves torn
1 tablespoon olive oil
salt and freshly ground black pepper
1 ripe avocado, peeled, pitted, and cut into chunks

Bring a large saucepan of water to the boil and add the pasta. Cook according to the package directions, but bite a piece a minute or so before the package says it will be ready to make sure you get it really al dente.

Drain the pasta in a colander, then return it to the still-warm saucepan and add the tomatoes, garlic, basil, olive oil and salt and pepper to taste. Swirl it around, then stir in the avocado chunks, and serve.

A spoonful of pesto makes a pleasant addition. Stir it in with the pasta before adding the tomatoes.

UNFILTERED COLD-PRESSED OLIVE OIL I adore this stuff—it's so green, so full of the flavor of olives. If you put some into a wide-necked jar or a bowl and chill it in the fridge for a few hours, it will become thick and you can then use it as a spread instead of butter—the purest and healthiest olive oil spread you could possibly get, and by far the best thing to put on your bread.

TAGLIATELLE WITH MUSHROOMS AND CREAM

Tagliatelle, mushrooms, and cream—you really can't go wrong; it's great comfort food, as far as I'm concerned. As to the type of milk or cream you use, that's up to you; if you use healthy soy milk for a guilt-free dish, I'd be surprised if anyone could tell the difference.

serves 2

9 ounces (250 g) tagliatelle
2 cups (250 g) Portobello or wild mushrooms
2 tablespoons olive oil
2–3 garlic cloves, chopped
1 tablespoon arrowroot or kuzu (*see page 159*)
1¼ cups (300 ml) light cream or soy milk
juice of ½ a lemon
dash of freshly grated nutmeg
salt and freshly ground black pepper

Bring a large saucepan of water to the boil and cook the tagliatelle according to the package directions.

Clean the mushrooms thoroughly, especially if you've included some wild ones. Slice them, if necessary, so they're roughly the same size. Heat the oil in a medium saucepan and add the mushrooms and garlic. Cook for 5–8 minutes, or until the mushrooms are tender.

Put the arrowroot or lumps of kuzu into a small bowl and add enough of the cream to make a pouring paste. Don't worry, the kuzu will soon become smooth once liquid is added.

Pour the rest of the cream into the pan with the mushrooms and bring to the boil, then pour in the arrowroot or kuzu paste. Stir over the heat for a minute or two until it thickens, then remove from the heat and stir in the lemon juice, grated nutmeg, and salt and pepper to taste.

Drain the pasta in a colander, then return it to the still-warm pan. Add the sauce, season to taste, and serve.

TAGLIATELLE WITH BROCCOLI CREAM SAUCE Use about 250 g (9 oz) broccoli florets instead of the mushrooms and garlic. Cook the broccoli in ½ inch (1 cm) boiling water for about 4 minutes, or until just tender, then drain. Mix the broccoli with the cream and the arrowroot or kuzu paste, as described above, season well and serve with the tagliatelle.

PAPPARDELLE WITH EGGPLANT AND ARTICHOKES

This is a useful recipe because it uses mainly store cabinet ingredients to make an excellent fast meal.

serves 4–5

1 pound 2 ounces (500 g) pappardelle
4 tablespoons olive oil
1 onion, minced
1 eggplant, diced
3–4 garlic cloves, minced
1 jar artichoke hearts
12 sun-dried tomatoes, roughly chopped
2 tablespoons capers, rinsed and drained
2 tablespoons pine nuts
salt and freshly ground black pepper
small handful of basil leaves, torn
Parmesan cheese, flaked or grated (optional)

Put a big saucepan of water on the stove to heat for the pasta. When it comes to the boil, add the pasta and cook for about 12 minutes, or according to the directions on the package, but bite a piece a minute or so before the package says it will be ready, to make sure you get it really al dente.

Meanwhile, heat 2 tablespoons of the oil in another pan and add the onion and eggplant. Cover and cook gently for 7 minutes, or until they are very nearly tender, then add the garlic, and cook for a further 1–2 minutes. Drain the artichoke hearts and add to the eggplant mixture, along with the sun-dried tomatoes and capers.

Toast the pine nuts by putting them under a hot broiler for a minute or two (watch carefully—they burn very quickly) or stirring them around in a dry saucepan over the heat until they're golden.

When the pasta is ready, drain it in a colander, then return it to the still-hot saucepan. Add the eggplant mixture and season well with salt and freshly ground black pepper. Serve on warmed plates, sprinkled with pine nuts and some torn basil leaves. Serve the Parmesan separately, if using.

PASTA TWIST, TOMATO, AND MOZZARELLA BAKE

This is quick to make, and once it's all mixed together it can be broiled and served immediately or kept ready for broiling or baking and serving later. It's a good dish for a crowd; just multiply everything up. I like to serve a crisp green salad with it.

serves 2

1 tablespoon olive oil
1 onion, minced
1 garlic clove, minced
2 cups (425 g) canned tomatoes in juice
⅔ cup (140 g) mozzarella cheese, drained and diced
½ cup (115 g) fresh Parmesan or Pecorino cheese, grated
salt and freshly ground black pepper
6 ounces (175 g) pasta twists (fusilli)

Heat the oil in a saucepan, add the onion, cover, and cook gently for 7 minutes. Then add the garlic and tomatoes, chopping them a little with a spoon. Stir and leave to cook, uncovered, for about 15 minutes, or until thick. Remove from the heat and stir in the mozzarella, half the Parmesan or Pecorino, and salt and pepper to taste.

Meanwhile, cook the pasta in a large pan of water according to the package directions, but bite a piece a minute or so before the package says it will be ready to make sure you get it really al dente. Drain the pasta then add it to the tomato mixture.

Pour into a shallow ovenproof dish and sprinkle with the rest of the Parmesan or Pecorino. Broil under a hot broiler for about 10 minutes until golden brown and bubbling.

You can make a vegan version by replacing the mozzarella with an extra tablespoon of olive oil and a handful of black olives, and topping the bake with grated vegan white cheese.

BROILED VEGETABLE LASAGNE

I must be honest, this dish is a rather time-consuming, though not difficult to make. I'm including it because it's a really useful dish that you can prepare in advance for a crowd—and because everyone always asks for it!

serves 4

1–2 zucchini, halved or quartered lengthwise
   and cut into 2-inch (5-cm) lengths
1 red onion, cut into sixths
1 eggplant, cut into chunks
1 tablespoon olive oil
1 tablespoon fresh lemon juice
salt
1 red and 1 yellow bell pepper, seeded and cut into strips
12 black olives
2 cups (425 g) canned artichoke hearts, drained and halved
8 ounces (225 g) lasagne sheets
small bunch of basil
2 cups (425 g) canned chopped tomatoes, in juice
freshly ground black pepper
3 × 4-ounce (115-g) pieces mozzarella cheese, drained and sliced
1 quantity Light and Creamy White Sauce (*see page 147*)
1/2 cup (115 g) grated Pecorino cheese

Heat the broiler to high. Put the zucchini, onion, and eggplant chunks onto a metal tray that will fit under your broiler. Sprinkle the vegetables with the olive oil, lemon juice, and a little salt, and move them around so that they are all evenly coated. I use my hands for this.

Add the pepper pieces to the tray—these don't need oiling. Broil for around 20 minutes, or until the vegetables are tender and browned in places, stirring them often. Stir in the black olives and artichoke hearts and set aside.

To assemble the dish, dip sheets of lasagne into cold water to soak them on both sides, then place a single layer to cover the base of a shallow ovenproof dish. Arrange half the vegetables on top, followed by a layer of basil leaves, half the tomatoes, a good seasoning of salt and pepper, half the mozzarella, another layer of lasagne, half the white sauce, and half the Pecorino. Repeat the layers—vegetables, basil, tomatoes, seasoning, mozzarella, lasagne, and a final layer of white sauce. Finish with the rest of the Pecorino.

Bake in a preheated 400°F (200°C) oven for 30 minutes, or until golden brown, bubbling, and fragrant.

BEANS AND LENTILS

BEANS AND LENTILS—LEGUMES OR PULSES—ARE RICH IN PROTEIN AND THE KIND OF CARBOHYDRATE YOU NEED FOR STEADY BLOOD SUGAR AND SUSTAINED ENERGY, ALONG WITH MANY OTHER VALUABLE NUTRIENTS. THEY'RE SIMPLE TO USE, AS THE FOLLOWING RECIPES DEMONSTRATE. APART FROM QUICK-COOKING LENTILS, WHICH ARE AS EASY TO PREPARE AS PASTA, I'VE USED CANNED BEANS IN MOST OF THE FOLLOWING RECIPES; I'VE ALSO GIVEN EQUIVALENT QUANTITIES FOR DRIED OR CANNED BEANS (*SEE PAGE 80*), IN CASE YOU WANT TO TRY MAKING A DISH FROM SCRATCH, STARTING WITH DRIED BEANS.

PREPARING DRIED BEANS AND LENTILS

Make sure the beans and lentils are fresh when you buy them. Although they have superb keeping qualities, they tend to dry out over time. Be especially selective with dried chickpeas, which can take forever to cook if they're old. It's worth spending a little more and getting top-quality ones.

Soaking

All dried beans, with the exception of lentils, need soaking before you cook them. You have two options: the long, cold soak or the short, hot soak. For the long, cold soak, cover the beans with plenty of cold water and leave to soak for 8 hours, or overnight.

For the short, hot soak, put the beans into a large, deep pot, cover with water as before, and heat. Boil for 2 minutes, then remove from the heat and leave to stand, covered, for 1 hour.

You can soak lentils too, if you wish, but it's not necessary. They'll just cook a little more quickly. Put them into a pan, cover with water—use the amount specified in the recipe if given, otherwise cover them with their height again—bring to the boil, and simmer until tender, 20–50 minutes depending on the type (see *opposite*).

Cooking

Always discard the soaking water, whether cold or hot, before cooking dried beans. After soaking, drain the beans in a colander, rinse under cold running water, return them to a saucepan, and barely cover with fresh water. Bring to the boil, and boil fast, uncovered, for 10 minutes; this is to destroy any enzymes that could cause stomach upsets. Then reduce the heat and let them simmer gently until tender (see *opposite*).

If you're making a dish using soaked but uncooked beans, be careful about what other ingredients you include. Salt and salty broths, as well as acidic ingredients such as tomatoes, and some spices, will cause the skins of the beans to toughen and prevent them from cooking properly. It's best to add these flavorings after the beans have softened.

Freezing

Cooked pulses freeze well. I find it convenient to cook 1 pound 2 ounces (500 g) of dried beans, then drain them and freeze them in portions of 1¼–1½ cups (300–350 g), which is the weight of the drained contents of a 15-ounce (425-g) can of beans. You will get five of these portions from 1 pound 2 ounces (500 g) dried beans.

Dried bean and canned bean equivalents

It's easy to convert a recipe from dried beans to canned beans and vice versa: ½ cup (115 g) dried beans is equivalent to a 15-ounce (425-g) can of beans, which, when drained, weighs about 10 ounces (300 g), around 1¼ cups.

Making beans digestible

There's no getting away from it—beans and lentils cause flatulence in many people. Pulses are so nutritious and delicious that it's a pity not to eat them because of this. I rather like Nigel Slater's comment: "So, beans give you wind. And what is wrong with that?" However, if this is a problem for you, it may be that all you need to do is add more salt to your dishes, because pulses produce magnesium in the gut, hence the wind, and salt, potassium, or something acidic like cider vinegar or fresh lemon juice, neutralizes it. You can also try adding spices or fennel seed for the same effect. That's one of the reasons why Indian recipes for pulses are so spicy. The Mexicans make extensive use of the herb called epazote, for the same purpose. It can be found in any Mexican grocery store and in supermarkets in neighborhoods with a large Mexican population.

COOKING TIMES

Pulses, soaked unless stated	Cooking time
Black beans	$1\frac{1}{4}$–$1\frac{1}{2}$ hours
Cannellini, pink, and California pink beans	$1\frac{1}{4}$–$1\frac{1}{2}$ hours
Chickpeas (garbanzo beans)	1–3 hours*
Flageolet beans	30 mins
Great white, northern, or navy beans	1 hour
Lentils, brown or green, unsoaked	50–60 mins
Lentils, gray-green, unsoaked	40–45 mins
Lentils, split red, Egyptian, unsoaked	15–20 mins
Lima beans	$1\frac{1}{4}$–$1\frac{1}{2}$ hours
Mung beans, unsoaked	35–45 mins
Mung bean dal (moong dal), unsoaked	15–20 mins
Red kidney beans	$1\frac{1}{4}$–$1\frac{1}{2}$ hours

*Some recipes suggest adding a pinch of baking soda to chickpeas (garbanzo beans) at the beginning of cooking to help them to soften. This destroys some of the B vitamins, though, so I prefer to be patient and cook them for a little longer.

GOLDEN LENTIL SOUP

One of the easiest, most nourishing, and comforting of soups. I add the garlic at the end in order to retain all its curative powers. This, along with the turmeric and lemon, makes it a fabulous soup for when you're not feeling so good (but it's one of my favorites for any time).

serves 4

2 onions, chopped
1 tablespoon olive oil
9 ounces (250 g) split red lentils
1 bay leaf
½ teaspoon turmeric powder
3 garlic cloves
1–2 tablespoons lemon juice
salt and freshly ground black pepper

Fry the onions gently in the olive oil in a large saucepan or pressure-cooker for 7–10 minutes, or until the onions are tender and just beginning to brown. Add the lentils, bay leaf, turmeric, and 5 cups (1.2 liters) water. Bring to the boil, then cook for 5 minutes on high pressure in a pressure-cooker, or simmer, covered, for 10–15 minutes, until the lentils are tender and pale.

Put the garlic in a food processor and process to chop (or crush the garlic, then put it into the food processor). Discard the bay leaf, pour the soup into the food processor, and process until smooth. Add more water if you want a thinner consistency, and stir in the lemon juice, and salt and pepper to taste.

For a spicier soup, add 1 teaspoon each of ground cumin and ground coriander to the pan along with the turmeric. Or, if you've got a sore throat, add a little chopped fresh or dried thyme to this soup and you'll feel better in no time.

LEEK, CHICKPEA, AND SAFFRON SOUP

This is such a lovely soup. It's very quick and easy to make, looks beautiful—shredded leeks and parsley, white and green in a clear golden broth, studded with plump chickpeas and flecked with deep orange saffron stamens—and tastes clean and light, yet at the same time it is warming and satisfying.

serves 4

½ tablespoon olive oil
9 ounces (250 g) leeks, finely sliced
a good pinch of saffron strands
2 cups (425 g) canned chickpeas
2 tablespoons flat-leaf parsley, roughly chopped
salt and freshly ground white pepper

Heat the oil in a large saucepan and add the leeks. Stir gently so that they all get coated with the oil, then cover and leave to cook for 4–5 minutes, but don't let them brown.

Add the saffron, chickpeas, and 2½ cups (600 ml) water. Bring to the boil, then reduce the heat, and leave to simmer gently for 5–10 minutes, or until the leeks are tender.

Stir in the chopped parsley, season, and serve.

LEEK, CHICKPEA, AND TURMERIC SOUP WITH LEMON Same color, different flavor—and less expensive. It's also particularly health giving because of the protective properties of turmeric (see page 56). Just add ½ teaspoon of turmeric instead of the saffron and stir in the juice of 1 lemon with the parsley.

BEANS AND LENTILS

PISTOU

A fast and easy version of a favorite Provençal stew. Very evocative of France—a bowlful of this and I'm practically there.

serves 3–4

2 large onions, minced
²⁄₃ cup (140 g) sugar snap peas or snow peas
3–4 zucchini, sliced
6 tomatoes (plum, if available), roughly chopped
4 garlic cloves, chopped
2 cups (480 g) canned navy or cannellini beans
2 teaspoons vegetable bouillon powder
salt and freshly ground black pepper

FOR THE PISTOU PURÉE
6 garlic cloves
2 tomatoes
handful of basil leaves
4 tablespoons olive oil

Put all the vegetables into a large saucepan with the garlic and the beans, together with their liquid. Pour in 2½ cups (600 ml) water, sprinkle with the bouillon powder, 1 teaspoon of salt, and a good grinding of black pepper. Simmer gently for around 30 minutes, or until the vegetables are very tender.

Meanwhile, make the pistou purée. Put the cloves of garlic into a food processor and process to chop, then add the tomatoes and basil, and process again. When smooth, add the oil, and process again.

Stir the pistou purée into the pan of vegetables, cook for a couple of minutes, then serve.

VEGETABLE BOUILLON POWDER Vegetable bouillon powder has become a real culinary star and is stocked in most supermarkets. Just mix with water, following the package instructions, to make stock or broth with an almost homemade flavor.

LENTIL AND BLACK OLIVE PÂTÉ

For this wonderful spread with a rich taste of olives, process together the drained contents of a 15-ounce (425-g) can of green or gray-green lentils, a small crushed garlic clove, 4 sun-dried tomatoes, ½–¾ cup (120–175 g) pitted black olives, and the juice of half a lemon. Season with freshly ground black pepper and salt, if necessary—very little is needed as the olives are already salty.

LIGHT AND CREAMY HUMMUS

This is so much tastier than store-bought and so easy to make. Simply drain a 15-ounce (425-g) can of chickpeas, reserving the liquid. Process the chickpeas in a food processor with 2 garlic cloves, the juice of a lemon, and a little salt, until the mixture is as smooth as possible, adding a little of the reserved chickpea liquid if necessary. Add 4 tablespoons of tahini and process again until gloriously smooth and creamy, adding more of the liquid as you go—you probably won't need it all. Stop when you reach your desired consistency— I love it like soft clouds of whipped cream. Serve in a bowl, or spread it out on a plate and sprinkle with a little paprika. You could also drizzle some olive oil over the top and decorate with a few olives, depending on what you're having with it.

TOFU SPREAD

This tastes rich and creamy, like a dairy-free version of garlic and herb cream cheese. Drain 1 cup or an 8-ounce (250-g) package of tofu, break it up roughly with your fingers, and put it into a food processor with several sprigs of flat-leaf parsley, a small crushed garlic clove, a squeeze of lemon juice, and a little salt and pepper. Process until creamy. Check the seasoning, adding more salt, pepper, and lemon juice if needed, then stir in 1 tablespoon of chopped chives or a finely chopped green onion (scallion).

AVOCADO DIP

This is avocado at its simplest and creamiest, almost like green mayonnaise or butter. Halve, pit, and peel a large, ripe avocado. Cut into rough chunks and process to a smooth cream in a food processor with 1 tablespoon of fresh lime or lemon juice, a few drops of Tabasco, and salt and pepper to taste. For more texture, mash the avocado and feel free to add other ingredients, such as chopped tomatoes, chili pepper, or coriander, for example.

MEDITERRANEAN BEAN PÂTÉ

This is very quick and easy to make and full of sunny flavors. Put the contents of a 15-ounce (425-g) can of cannellini, pinto, or California pink beans into a food processor with the juice of half a lemon, 3–4 sun-dried tomatoes, and a small handful of pitted black olives, and process to a thick, chunky paste. Season with salt and pepper and tear some fresh basil leaves over the top. This is great in sandwiches, as a dip with raw vegetables or crisp toast, or on a plate with salad leaves and ripe tomatoes for a light meal.

BABA GHANOUJ (EGGPLANT DIP)

This delectable, addictive, pale smoky cream is wonderful with raw vegetables, warm bread, or salad. Prick 3 eggplant in several places, then put them on a rack in a hot oven, or arranged on the stovetop over gas burners (watch carefully if you choose this method) or under a very hot broiler. For best results, the skins of the eggplant need to be well charred. This takes 25–30 minutes and you'll have to turn them frequently, using tongs. Cool the eggplant slightly, then peel off the charred skin—it will come off easily in long strips. Process the eggplant to a pale cream with 2 crushed garlic cloves, 3 tablespoons tahini, 3 tablespoons olive oil, and 3 tablespoons lemon juice. Season with salt and pepper to taste, adding more lemon juice, if necessary.

BEAN SALAD NIÇOISE

This is a delicious salad that always makes me think of vacations and sunshine. I love it for lunch, with some warm bread or hot pasta, just tossed in olive oil, with perhaps a little soft goat cheese. It's also good as an appetizer, in which case it will feed four.

serves 2–4

1 cup (250 g) thin green beans
1¾ cups (400 g) canned flageolet, great northern, or navy beans
1 cup (250 g) tomatoes, plum if available
few sprigs of basil
handful of black olives
salt and freshly ground black pepper

FOR THE MUSTARD DRESSING
1 teaspoon Dijon mustard
½ a garlic clove, crushed
1 tablespoon red wine vinegar or cider vinegar
3 tablespoons olive oil

Trim the green beans—I like to take off the tops and leave the little curly "tails." Cook them in boiling water for 4–6 minutes, or until tender but still crunchy. Drain in a colander and cool under cold running water. Drain again.

While they're cooking, drain and rinse the flageolet or white beans, cut the tomatoes into chunky pieces, tear the basil, and put them all into a bowl, along with the olives. Add the green beans and season with salt and a little pepper.

For the dressing, put the mustard, garlic, vinegar, and a little salt into a bowl and mix with a fork or small whisk, then gradually whisk in the oil. Season to taste.

Add half the dressing to the salad and toss so that it's all glossy, then heap it onto plates or a serving platter, and sprinkle the rest of the dressing over and around the beans. Grind some more pepper over the beans before serving.

LENTIL AND CUMIN CAKES WITH MINTY RAITA

These make a pleasant appetizer or side dish for an Indian meal,
but they can also stand alone as an entrée. Children love them.
My mother used to give them to them to me with mint sauce, but these
days I prefer them with a minty raita.

makes about 16

> **1 cup (250 g) red lentils**
> **1 onion, minced**
> **2 garlic cloves, minced**
> **2 teaspoons cumin seeds**
> **5 tablespoons canola oil**
> **salt and freshly ground black pepper**
> **3–4 tablespoons gram flour (see page 102), for coating**
> **1 quantity Raita (see page 67), made with mint**

Put the lentils into a saucepan with 2 cups (500 ml) water and bring to the boil, then cook gently for about 15 minutes, or until the lentils are soft and pale gold and no water remains. Remove from the heat, cover, and leave for 10–15 minutes to continue to cook and dry in the residual heat.

Meanwhile, in another saucepan, sauté the onion, garlic, and cumin gently in 1 tablespoon of the oil, for 7–8 minutes, or until the onion is tender. Add the onion mixture to the lentils, mashing them with a wooden spoon. Season with plenty of salt and pepper to taste.

Put some of the gram flour on a plate. Take Ping-Pong ball–sized pieces of the lentil mixture, drop them into the gram flour. Sprinkle them with more gram flour, and form into small, flat cakes, pressing them together firmly.

Heat the remaining oil in a skillet and sauté the cakes until they are golden brown and crisp on one side, then turn them over with a spatula and fry them on the other side. Drain them on paper towels when they're done. Alternatively, brush them with oil on both sides and broil or bake in the oven, turning them to brown both sides. Serve with the Raita.

CHICKPEA, TOMATO, AND CORIANDER SALAD

You can make this filling and nutritious snack in about five minutes. I like to scoop it up with crisp Little Gem or romaine lettuce leaves, but you could pack it into a pita bread, or if you want to make it even more nutritious, serve it with Tahini Sauce (*see page 147*) which is very quick to prepare and goes very well with it.

serves 2

2 cups (425 g) canned chickpeas, drained
4 tomatoes, chopped
1 green onion (scallion), chopped
1 small garlic clove, crushed
squeeze of lemon juice
few sprigs of fresh coriander (cilantro), chopped
drizzle of extra virgin olive oil (optional)

Mix all the ingredients together, and drizzle with the olive oil, if using.

FRENCH WHITE BEAN AND HERB SALAD Use a can of cannellini, navy, or great white northern beans instead of the chickpeas. Leave out the tomatoes, and instead of the coriander use 2–3 tablespoons of chopped summer herbs—parsley makes a good base, plus a little of anything else available that takes your fancy—mint, tarragon, lovage, fennel, rosemary, or thyme.

PUY LENTIL SALAD Follow the French White Bean and Herb Salad recipe, using either a can of gray-green lentils instead of the white beans, or ½ cup (115 g) dried lentils cooked as described on page 80.

THAI BEAN CAKES WITH SWEET RED PEPPER SAUCE

Well, I thought, people make Thai crab cakes, so why not use the same
flavorings to make Thai bean cakes? It works!

serves 4 as an appetizer, 2 as a light entrée

FOR THE RED PEPPER DIPPING SAUCE
1 red bell pepper
pinch of dried chili pepper flakes
1 tablespoon apple juice concentrate
1 teaspoon rice vinegar or cider vinegar
salt and freshly ground black pepper

2 cups (425 g) canned cannellini, pinto, or California pink beans
1 large green onion (scallion), chopped
around ½ cup (50 g) coriander (cilantro) leaves, roughly chopped
2 teaspoons Thai red curry paste
1 dried lime leaf, crumbled, stem discarded
1 tablespoon gram flour (see *page 102*)
1–2 tablespoons olive oil
lime wedges, to serve

Start by making the sauce. Using a potato peeler, remove as much of the shiny skin of the bell pepper as you can, although there's no need to be too careful. Then halve, seed, and finely chop the pepper. Put into a saucepan with the chili pepper flakes, the apple juice concentrate, and vinegar and simmer, uncovered, for about 15 minutes, or until the pepper is tender. Season with salt and pepper.

Drain the beans in a sieve, then rinse them under cold running water. Blot thoroughly with paper towels so they're fairly dry. Then put them into a food processor with the green onion, coriander, Thai red curry paste, lime leaf, salt, and freshly ground black pepper, and process briefly until you have a chunky purée that clings together.

Divide the mixture into four—or, if you're serving the cakes as an appetizer and have the patience, eight—form into flat cakes and coat with the gram flour. Heat the olive oil in a skillet and fry the cakes on both sides until golden. Serve immediately with the dipping sauce and lime wedges.

VEGETABLE TEMPURA

Crisp, golden tempura are a delicious treat. These are easy to make and quite nutritious, since gram flour is used in the batter. Serve them, oriental-style, with a dipping sauce and a little pile of grated raw turnip or daikon (which is said to help digest the oil), or with Tartar Sauce (*see page 146*) for a Western approach.

serves 4 as an appetizer, 2 as an entrée

FOR THE DIPPING SAUCE AND ACCOMPANIMENTS
1 tablespoon grated fresh ginger
1 tablespoon soy sauce
1 tablespoon mirin, apple juice concentrate, or honey
1 tablespoon rice vinegar
1-inch (5-cm) slice daikon or 1 turnip, peeled and grated
sprinkling of sesame seeds

canola oil for deep-frying
1 cup (115 g) gram flour (*see page 102*)
1 cup (115 g) self-rising flour or arrowroot (*see page 159*)
1 teaspoon baking powder, or 2 teaspoons if you're using arrowroot
½ teaspoon salt
1¼ cups (300 ml) ice-cold club soda or sparkling mineral water
2 cups (450 g) assorted vegetables, in bite-size pieces: broccoli florets, snow peas, green or wax beans, red onion, red bell pepper, asparagus spears, green onions (scallions)

Heat the oil for deep-frying.

First make the dipping sauce. Squeeze the ginger with your fingers over a small bowl to catch the golden juice. Discard the rest of the ginger and mix the soy sauce, mirin, apple juice concentrate or honey, and the rice vinegar with the ginger juice. Set aside, along with the grated daikon or turnip in another small bowl, garnished with a sprinkling of sesame seeds.

Put the gram flour into a bowl with the self-rising flour or arrowroot, baking powder, and salt. Add the club soda or sparkling mineral water, beating all the time—though a few little lumps don't matter for tempura batter.

When the oil is hot enough to sizzle and form bubbles when a wooden chopstick or wooden spoon handle are dipped into it, start coating the vegetables with the batter, then drop them into the oil. Don't cook too many at once—just enough to cover the surface of the oil. Fry for around 4 minutes, flipping them over if the tops seem to be less golden, then remove from the oil with a slotted spoon and drain on paper towels. Continue until all the vegetables are done, then serve immediately with the dipping sauce and accompaniments.

GREEK LIMA BEANS

Have you eaten these, or something similar, at a harborside *taverna* on a Greek island one warm summer's evening, the air full of the scent of wild thyme and the buzzing of cicadas? Forgive me for getting carried away.... Anyway, this is a quick version of the dish, using canned lima beans and sun-dried tomato paste. It gives similar results, but no *taverna* or harbor lights—sorry! These beans are useful for serving with all kinds of other foods. They turn a bowl of leafy salad into a lunch; they're great served alongside some fluffy grains, or scooped up with crusty bread; or eat them with some baby new potatoes cooked in their skins, tossed in olive oil, and sprinkled with chopped mint, along with a green salad.

serves 2–4

I onion, minced
I tablespoon olive oil
I garlic clove, sliced
2 cups (425 g) canned lima beans (in salted water, not sweetened), drained
I tablespoon sun-dried tomato paste
juice of ½ a lemon
salt and freshly ground black pepper
fresh parsley, thyme, or basil, chopped

Fry the onion in the oil for 5 minutes, add the garlic, and fry for an additional 5 minutes.

Stir in the lima beans, sun-dried tomato paste, lemon juice, and salt and pepper to taste. If you use good-quality sun-dried tomato paste, it doesn't need any more cooking. Remove from the heat and stir in some chopped parsley, thyme, or basil. Let it stand for as long as possible for the flavors to develop. Serve warm or cold, as you like.

SLOW-COOKED BLACK BEANS

Although I'm a great one for saving time by using canned beans, there are certain recipes that I really love to make with dried beans, and this is one of them. It really isn't any trouble—I just do a "quick soak" rather than overnight, and then you just leave them to cook. At some point, sauté the onions, cook a pot of rice if you want, prepare the toppings in a relaxed way—and that's it! This is deeply satisfying food that everyone loves, and one of those dishes that tastes even better when reheated the next day.

serves 4–6

2½ cups (500 g) black beans
2 large onions, chopped
2 tablespoons olive oil
1 tablespoon cumin seeds
6 garlic cloves, chopped
juice of 1 lemon or lime
salt and freshly ground black pepper

TO SERVE
⅔ cup (142 ml) sour cream
bunch of fresh coriander (cilantro), roughly chopped
1–2 large red chili peppers, sliced, with or without seeds
1 avocado, chopped (optional)
hot cooked rice (see *page 111*), or bread or tortilla chips

Put the beans into a large pan and cover with cold water by around 2 inches (5 cm). Soak overnight or boil for 2 minutes, then leave to stand for 1 hour (see *page 80*). Drain, add enough fresh water to cover the beans, bring to the boil, and cook at a rolling boil for 10 minutes. Reduce the heat, cover, and leave to cook for 1¼–1½ hours, or until the beans are really tender, adding a little more water if necessary.

Meanwhile, sauté the onions in the oil for 10 minutes. Add the cumin and garlic and cook for another 2 minutes. Set aside.

When the beans are done, stir in the onions. Then remove around a quarter of the mixture and mash thoroughly or purée in a food processor. Put back with the rest of the beans and stir well, adding more water if necessary, the lemon or lime juice and plenty of salt and pepper.

Reheat, then top with a swirl of sour cream and a scattering of coriander, chili pepper, and avocado, if using, or put these toppings into bowls along with the rice, bread, or whatever else is being offered and let people help themselves. I like to serve the beans with a leafy salad with mustard dressing.

BEST-EVER CHILI

This is quick and easy to make, filling, totally healthy, inexpensive, and very tasty. It's particularly good served over Idaho potatoes that have been baked until their skins are really crisp. They need to go into a hot oven (450°F/230°C) 1–1½ hours before you want to eat—but if you want to get the chili to the table faster, chunks of warm bread or a quickly cooked grain (see page 111) are excellent, too.

serves 3–4

1 onion, chopped
1 large red bell pepper, seeded and chopped
2 garlic cloves, minced
1 mild red chili pepper, seeded and finely chopped, or red chili pepper flakes, to taste
1 tablespoon olive oil
1 teaspoon ground coriander
2 cups (425 g) canned green lentils, drained
2 cups (425 g) canned red kidney beans, drained
2 cups (425 g) canned chopped tomatoes
salt and freshly ground black pepper

TO SERVE
bunch of fresh coriander (cilantro), roughly chopped
⅔ cup (142 ml) sour cream
1 avocado, chopped (optional)

To make the chili, cook the onion, red pepper, garlic, and chili pepper in the oil in a large covered saucepan for 15–20 minutes, or until the vegetables are tender. Stir them from time to time to prevent them from sticking.

Add the ground coriander, lentils, red kidney beans, and tomatoes and mix well. Leave to simmer gently for 10 minutes, season, then serve with your chosen accompaniments and garnishes.

SPECIAL MEALS

CHRISTMAS

FORK SUPPER WITH AN INDIAN FLAVOR

SUMMER BARBECUE

Lentil and Black Olive Pâté (*see page 86*) with raw vegetables

Oatcakes (*see page 129*)

Tofu and Mushroom Skewers (*see page 144*)

Cumin-roasted Sweet Potatoes (*see page 42*)

Tempeh Burgers (*see page 151*) with Tartar Sauce (*see page 146*)

Little Gem, Chicory, and Watercress Salad (*see page 33*)

Lemon Cake (*page 184*) or Vegan Victoria Sandwich Cake (*see page 186*)

Summer Berry Compote (*see page 175*)

DRINKS PARTY

Marinated Olives (*see page 34*)

Vegetarian Sushi (*see page 120*)

Avocado Dip (*see page 87*) with raw vegetables

Deep-fried Tofu and Hijiki Balls (*see page 160*)

Vegetable Tempura (*see page 94*)

Tartar Sauce (*see page 146*)

LITTLE PROVENÇAL PANCAKES

Make these as dollar pancakes for an impressive but easy appetizer, or
make them larger, to use as a burrito-style wrap for snacks.

makes around 16 dollar pancakes

> **2 cups (225 g) chickpea flour or gram flour (*see below*)**
> **1 teaspoon salt**
> **1 teaspoon baking powder**
> **2 teaspoons cumin seeds**
> **a little olive oil for frying**
> **handful of fresh coriander (cilantro), chopped**
>
> **FOR THE SALSA TOPPING**
> **1 beefsteak tomato, quite finely chopped**
> **2 green onions (scallions), chopped**
> **1 tablespoon lemon juice**

Measure out 1¼–2 cups (300–450 ml) water and set aside. Sift the gram flour into a bowl with the salt
and baking powder. Add the cumin seeds, then start pouring in the water, stirring all the time. Once
you've got a fairly thick paste, stop pouring and beat to remove all the lumps, or as many as you can,
then continue stirring the water into the paste until you've got a consistency like light cream.

To make the salsa, mix together all the ingredients and set aside.

To fry the dollar pancakes, warm 1 teaspoon of olive oil in a skillet, then pour in a good tablespoonful of
batter to make a little pancake. Put another in beside it, leaving some space between them. When the
base looks set and little holes are appearing on top, flip each pancake over with a metal spatula and
cook the other side. Keep them warm while you repeat the process to make the rest, then top each
with a spoonful of salsa and some chopped coriander, and eat immediately, while they're light and
fragrant.

CHICKPEA OR GRAM FLOUR This is a light golden flour which has all the nutrients of
chickpeas and a low glycemic index rating. It makes beautiful pancakes and can be used to thicken bean
mixtures. You can also use it to coat fritters, either as it is, instead of flour, or mixed to a thin paste with
water and used instead of beaten egg. Dip the fritters into the diluted gram flour then into more gram
flour or bread crumbs before frying.

ZUCCHINI KOFTAS

Serve these crisp and tasty morsels with this sauce—or with Fresh Tomato and Coriander Chutney (*see page 66*)—as an appetizer, or add some hot cooked rice to make a light entrée.

serves 4 as an appetizer, 2 as an entrée

FOR THE SAUCE
2 teaspoons olive oil
I onion, minced
2 garlic cloves, crushed
2 teaspoons fresh ginger, grated
6 fresh curry leaves or ½ teaspoon curry powder
2 beefsteak tomatoes, chopped
salt and freshly ground black pepper

3 cups (750 g) zucchini, grated
I medium onion, minced
I cup (115 g) gram flour (*see page 102*)
I teaspoon red chili pepper flakes
½ teaspoon baking powder
I teaspoon salt
3 tablespoons fresh coriander (cilantro) or mint, chopped
canola oil, for frying

First make the sauce. Heat the oil in a saucepan, add the onion, and fry gently for 5 minutes. Then add the garlic, ginger, and curry leaves or powder, and cook for an additional 5 minutes, or until the onion is tender. Add the tomatoes and leave to cook gently for around 10 minutes, or until the tomatoes are softened, then add salt and pepper to taste.

While the sauce is simmering, make the koftas. Squeeze the excess juice from the zucchini, then mix with all the other ingredients, except the oil.

Just before you're ready to serve the meal—because koftas are best eaten hot, sizzling, and crisp—heat ½ inch (1 cm) canola oil in a sauté pan or wok.

Drop straggly, slightly flattened, walnut-sized chunks of the kofta mixture into the oil and fry for 2–3 minutes, or until they're brown on one side, then flip them over and cook the other side. Make sure they're really brown and crisp, then lift them out with a slotted spoon, and drain on paper towels. Serve with the sauce.

LENTIL DAL

This wonderful spicy sauce is so easy to make and a great way of adding protein and interest to a simple plate of vegetables or grains. I love it and make it often, sometimes varying it by adding a fried onion with the remaining spices, or topping it with a crunchy garnish of chopped garlic fried in 2–3 tablespoons of oil.

serves 4

**1 cup (250 g) split red lentils
1 large onion, chopped
1 bay leaf
½ teaspoon turmeric powder
1 tablespoon fresh ginger, grated
2 teaspoons ground cumin
2 teaspoons ground coriander
3 garlic cloves, crushed
juice of 1 lemon
salt and freshly ground black pepper**

Put the lentils into a large saucepan with the onion, bay leaf, turmeric, ginger, and 3½ cups (900 ml) water. Bring to the boil and simmer for 20 minutes, or until the lentils are tender and pale. Remove and discard the bay leaf.

Put the cumin and coriander into a small saucepan and stir over the heat for a few seconds, until they smell aromatic and fragrant, then stir them into the dal.

Add the garlic and lemon juice and season with salt and pepper to taste.

LEMONS Lemons must be one of the most useful flavorings; their fresh sharpness complements so many other ingredients, and they are also extremely appealing in its own right. Always use freshly squeezed lemon juice, both for its flavor and its health-giving properties—it's a wonderful source of vitamin C, supports the immune system, and has liver-cleansing properties.

MIDDLE EASTERN LENTILS AND SPINACH

Who would think that such inexpensive and simple foods could taste so good and be so deeply satisfying? This is such a comforting dish, too, and packed with iron and all kinds of other good things. Serve it on its own, or with a cooked grain for a perfectly balanced meal. Any leftovers will taste great cold.

serves 4

1 tablespoon olive oil
1 onion, sliced
1 teaspoon ground coriander
1 teaspoon ground cumin
6 cups (500 g) spinach
2 × 15-ounce (425-g) cans gray-green or green lentils, drained
2 garlic cloves, crushed
juice of ½ a lemon
salt and freshly ground black pepper

Heat the olive oil in a large saucepan, add the onion, and cook gently for around 7 minutes, or until tender.

Add the coriander and cumin and stir for a few seconds over the heat as the aroma is released, then add the spinach. Continue to cook for around 10 minutes, as the spinach shrinks and becomes tender. You could cut it a few times with the end of a metal spatula and move it around to help it to cook evenly.

When the spinach is done, add the lentils, and cook gently for a few minutes until they're hot. Then stir in the garlic, lemon juice, and salt and pepper to taste.

GARLIC Garlic as a flavoring needs no introduction, and its therapeutic properties are well documented. It's a potent natural remedy that, unlike the antibiotics you get from the doctor, only kills off the bad bacteria, so you've still got the friendly ones that you need to keep you healthy. It also seems to help stop the spread of cancer. Over time, I've found myself using more and more of it, and chopping or slicing rather than crushing it. I've recently realized, however, that to get the full benefit of garlic's health-giving properties, you have to use it raw or only barely heated. So recently I've gone back to crushing it (or, to be specific, grating it), then adding it to food at the end of cooking.

PUY LENTIL CASSEROLE

This is simple, warming, and delicious, with a taste of the south of France around it. I like it just as it is, though you could serve it with bread, potato, or a cooked grain.

serves 4

1 tablespoon olive oil
1 onion, peeled and chopped
1 pound 2 ounces (500 g) leeks
1 pound 2 ounces (500 g) carrots
2 bay leaves
2–3 sprigs of thyme or rosemary
1 cup (250 g) gray-green lentils
2 cups (425 g) canned chopped tomatoes
3–4 garlic cloves, crushed
salt and freshly ground black pepper
extra olive oil and chopped parsley (optional)

Warm the olive oil in a large saucepan, add the onion, and cook gently, covered, for 7 minutes.

Meanwhile, wash and trim the leeks as necessary and cut into 1-inch (2.5-cm) lengths. Scrub or scrape the carrots and slice them. Add these vegetables to the pan along with the bay leaves and thyme or rosemary, and leave to cook gently for an additional 4–5 minutes.

Stir in the lentils and add 2½ cups (1 liter) water. Bring to the boil, then cover and leave to cook for around 30 minutes, or until the lentils and vegetables are tender.

Add the tomatoes, mix, and leave to cook for an additional 10–15 minutes. Stir in the garlic, and season to taste with salt and pepper just before serving.

Some good-quality olive oil drizzled over the top of this bean stew is excellent, as is a final garnish of chopped parsley—but it's also very good without.

CEREAL GRAINS

CEREAL GRAINS ARE A GREAT SOURCE OF NUTRIENTS AND HAVE A VALUABLE AND DELICIOUS PART TO PLAY IN A HEALTHY, BALANCED VEGETARIAN DIET. DON'T CONFUSE WHOLE GRAINS WITH OTHER FORMS OF CARBOHYDRATE, SUCH AS WHITE FLOUR AND BREAD, AND SHUN THEM BECAUSE THEY'RE "HIGH IN CARBOHYDRATE." UNLIKE REFINED WHITE FLOUR AND PRODUCTS MADE FROM IT, WHOLE GRAINS AND THEIR FLOURS, AS WELL AS PROVIDING A WIDE RANGE OF VITAMINS, MINERALS, PROTEIN, AND FIBER, HAVE A LOW GLYCEMIC INDEX RATING (*SEE PAGE 9*), WHICH MEANS THEY'LL HELP YOU GET SLIM AND STAY SLIM.

CEREAL GRAINS

Amaranth

Like quinoa (*see below*), amaranth contains complete protein and it is high in calcium. It's also very digestible, but it's difficult to use because the tiny sand-like grains cook to a mush and have rather a strong flavor. Try adding a tablespoon or two of amaranth to other grains when you're cooking them to increase the nutritional value; or better still, buy amaranth in its "popped" form, then add the yummy doll-sized "popcorn" to muesli or granola (*see page 118*) or stir it into yogurt.

Barley

One of the reasons I love barley is that it's a grain which grows in our colder northern climates as well as in hot, dry places. It's also so modest and unassuming, yet nourishing and sweet tasting. I like to use organic pearl barley, which, though "polished," still has more fiber than brown rice. Barley flour is available from health food and whole food stores and I love to use it for baking. I agree with Elizabeth David who said, "Those who acquire a taste for it are likely to become addicts. I am one." So am I.

Buckwheat

Buckwheat is such a lovely grain—or, technically, a seed—and, I think, greatly underused. It's particularly good for the old and the young because it's very easy to digest (it's better in this respect than rice), and for women because it's a rich source of some of the nutrients that women tend to lack, such as magnesium, zinc, vitamin B$_6$, iron, folic acid, and calcium. It also contains rutin, which is helpful for high blood pressure and varicose veins. In this book you'll find recipes for using the grain and also for buckwheat noodles (*see pages 60 and 62*).

Millet

Golden millet, which cooks to a fluffy consistency and, if you roast it as suggested, tastes delicately nutty, contains more protein and iron than most grains (though quinoa and amaranth have the most protein), plus potassium, magnesium, and phosphorous. It's also easier to digest than most grains.

Oats

There's something sensual and soothing about the flavor and creamy consistency of oats. I use organic rolled oats for oatmeal and muesli mixes, oat bran and germ to stir into soy yogurt for my current favorite breakfast, and medium or fine oatmeal for baking. All are delicious.

Quinoa

Confusingly pronounced "keen-wa," quinoa, a traditional grain from Mexico, is exceptional because weight for weight it contains more protein than meat and is a useful source of calcium. It also has a very low glycemic index rating (*see page 9*), so will sustain you without sending your blood sugar racing. Along with millet and buckwheat, it makes an excellent healthy alternative to couscous. It's also available "popped," to add to muesli or granola.

Rice

I like to use organic short-grain brown rice, which you'll have to go to a specialty health food store to get. It is by far the most delicious type of brown rice and a very cleansing, healing grain. It's great for any kind of detox program, as well as for everyday use. I also love fragrant basmati rice and use both the white and brown varieties, each of which has a fairy low glycemic index rating (see *page 9*), although the brown variety has more nutrients. Basmati is a long-grain rice, originally from Pakistan, now also grown in Texas.

Wild rice

Technically a seed, though treated as a grain, wild rice has a delicious, smoky flavor, a chewy texture, and a certain elegance. I love it mixed with rice.

COOKING GRAINS

When buying grains by weight, remember that 8 ounces (225 g) of grain is the weight of 1 cup of most grains. When cooked, grains roughly triple in weight and volume.

One cup of:	Cups of liquid	Cooking time	Notes
Barley, organic pearl	2–3	20–30 mins	Grains look plump and juicy and are tender when done.
Buckwheat	2	15 mins	Buy untoasted organic and toast in pan as described on page 130. Add water, bring to boil, cover, and leave to stand for 15 mins, until grains are tender but still intact. Stir gently.
Millet	3	15–20 mins	Stir grains in a dry pan over heat for 4–5 mins, until they smell toasted, then pour in water, and cook. Grains look pale and are tender when done. Leave to stand, covered, for 10 mins to "fluff."
Quinoa	2	12–15 mins	Grains look pearly with "Saturn" ring when done. Leave to stand, covered, for 10 mins to "fluff."
Rice, brown organic	2–2½	40–45 mins	Grains are swollen and tender, with a slightly creamy texture when done. Leave to stand, still covered, for 10–15 mins, then stir gently with a fork.
Rice, brown basmati	2	30 mins	Grains are tender but separate and with some bite when done. Leave to stand, still covered, for 10–15 mins, then stir gently with a fork.
Rice, white basmati	2	13–15 mins	Grains are tender and separate when done. Leave to stand, covered, for 5 mins, then stir gently with a fork.
Wild rice	4	45–50 mins	Grains split when tender, showing white insides.

IDEAS FOR USING CEREAL GRAINS

It's always worth cooking more grains than you need; with some cooked grains in the refrigerator, the next meal is never more than a few minutes away. All these recipes serve 3–4 people.

Stuffed peppers
Preheat the oven to 375°F (190°C). Mix ¾ cup (175 g) of any cooked grain—I recommend quinoa—with a small onion, chopped and fried with a crushed garlic clove, 2 chopped sun-dried tomatoes, 2–3 tablespoons toasted pine nuts and the same of raisins, or 1 tablespoon capers, and season to taste with salt, freshly ground black pepper, and a good pinch of ground cinnamon. Cut the tops off 2 red bell peppers, scoop out the seeds, fill them with this mixture, and bake for 20–30 minutes in an oiled dish.

Asian grains
Flavor 1½ cups (350 g) cooked grains—buckwheat is especially good—with 1–2 tablespoons soy sauce and stir in 2–3 chopped green onions (scallions), 1 heaping tablespoon hijiki or arame seaweed (*prepared as described on page 122*), and 1 tablespoon toasted sesame seeds. Drain and dice 1 cup (250 g) tofu, toss in 1 tablespoon soy sauce, 1 teaspoon of grated fresh ginger, and a crushed or grated garlic clove, and stir into the grains. Alternatively, drain, pat dry, and very thinly slice 1 cup (250 g) smoked tofu, sauté in a little oil until crisp on both sides, drain, and add to the grains. Tahini Sauce (*see page 147*) goes well with this dish.

Mediterranean grains
Fry a minced onion and a diced eggplant in 2 tablespoons of olive oil for 10 minutes until tender, then add a 2 cups (425 g) canned tomatoes and 2 crushed garlic cloves and cook for another 10–15 minutes. Mix with 1½ cups (350 g) cooked grains—millet, quinoa, buckwheat, or rice. Add a small handful of black olives, 2 or 3 sprigs of chopped basil, 3–4 chopped sun-dried tomatoes, salt, and freshly ground black pepper to taste. You could also stir in a 2 cups (425 g) canned chickpeas, drained, or add a small handful of toasted pine nuts.

Mushroom grains
Wash 4–6 large mushroom caps (such as Portobellos) and brush the white sides lightly with olive oil. Broil, gill-side down, for 5–10 minutes until nearly tender, then turn them over, season, and broil until they weep black juice (no need to oil unless you want to). Serve with 1½ cups (350 g) cooked grains—they're terrific with buckwheat—and 2 cups (250 g) spinach, cooked in a dry saucepan, then drained and seasoned with salt, freshly ground black pepper, and grated nutmeg.

Alternatively, sauté 2 cups (250 g) nice firm Portobello mushrooms (sliced if large) in 2–3 tablespoons of olive oil for 5 minutes, until tender, then fork through the grains with 1–2 crushed garlic cloves and salt and pepper to taste.

Grain salads

Any cooked grain makes the basis of a delicious salad, and you can really throw in anything you fancy. Starting with 2 cups (450 g) cooked grains, try adding 2 cups (425 g) canned chickpeas, drained, together with a handful of black or green olives and 2–3 crushed cloves of garlic; or try adding 1 cup (115 g) toasted cashew nuts, toasted almonds, or toasted pine nuts, a broiled red bell pepper, roughly chopped, and a small handful of juicy raisins (soaked for a few minutes in hot water to plump if necessary). Or mix in a handful of grated carrot or raw beet, a swirl of olive oil, a squeeze of lemon juice, a small handful of minced parsley, then stir a small handful of pumpkin (pepitas) or sunflower seeds in a dry saucepan for a minute or two and pour them, hot and sizzling, on top. Serve any of these with a creamy dip and some green leaves for a delicious and energizing meal.

Middle Eastern grains

Fry a sliced onion in olive oil for 7 minutes, or until tender, then stir in 1 teaspoon cumin seeds—or to taste—and perhaps the same of ground coriander, along with 1–2 minced garlic cloves. Stir this mixture into 1½ cups (350 g) hot cooked grains—brown basmati rice is good—along with 2–3 tablespoons of toasted almonds, pine nuts, or cashew nuts, and 2 cups (425 g) canned chickpeas or lentils, drained, or 1 cup (225 g) lightly cooked frozen fava beans. Season with salt and pepper and scatter with chopped fresh coriander (cilantro), if available.

Grain burgers

Mix 1½ cups (350 g) cooked grains, such as brown rice, millet, or quinoa, with enough nut butter (organic peanut, almond, or hazelnut butter, or tahini) to bind them—about 4–6 tablespoons. Stir in 1–2 crushed garlic cloves, 1–2 teaspoons grated fresh ginger, and a dash of soy sauce, if you like. Season with salt and pepper. Form into 6–8 patties, pressing them together well. Brush with canola or olive oil and broil for around 6 minutes or sauté in 2–3 tablespoons of hot canola oil until crisp and brown on both sides.

SALT Recently, I've started using the most natural and unrefined salt you can buy. It's often called Celtic sea salt (also known as *gros sel*), and is widely used in France. It looks rather gray and damp in the package—you almost think you might see a piece of seaweed lurking there! But it's full of natural minerals, including iodine, so it's a very balanced salt, recommended by therapists, and it's also bursting with flavor—quite the tastiest salt available. Because it's rather damp, I spread it out thinly on a cookie sheet and dry it over a radiator for a few hours (or you could use a cool oven), then grind it in a coffee grinder. This is better than using a salt mill—or at least all the ones I've tried—because they become clogged with the salt as it's so moist.

GOLDEN RICE, AVOCADOS, AND WILD MUSHROOMS

This consists of a protein-rich mixture of rice and split red lentils, served with avocados, wild mushrooms, and garlic. Everyone loves this combination, though either part—the rice and lentils, or the stuffed avocados—can be used separately.

serves 4

1 cup (250 g) basmati and wild rice mix
½ cup (125 g) split red lentils
¼ teaspoon turmeric
6 cups (500 g) assorted wild mushrooms, cleaned
1 tablespoon olive oil
2 garlic cloves, minced
juice of ½ a lemon, plus an extra squeeze
salt and freshly ground black pepper
2 avocados

Preheat the oven to 300°F (150°C).

Put the rice and lentils into a saucepan with the turmeric and 2½ cups (600 ml) water. Bring to the boil, then cover and leave to cook for 15 minutes. Remove from the heat and leave, still covered, for 5 minutes.

Sauté the wild mushrooms in the oil in a large saucepan for 5–10 minutes, or until tender, adding the garlic and a squeeze of lemon juice toward the end of the cooking time. Season with salt and pepper.

Halve, pit, and peel the avocados, coat on both sides with lemon juice and season with salt and pepper. Add the remaining lemon juice to the rice and lentil mixture—it will immediately brighten the color.

Fluff the rice and lentils with a fork, adding a little salt, then spread on a serving platter. Top with the avocado halves, cut-sides upward. Spoon the mushrooms onto them, heaping them up but leaving a rim of green showing. Leave in the oven for up to 15 minutes while you eat your appetizer, but don't let the avocados get too hot—warmed is fine, but don't let them bake, or they'll spoil.

CEREAL GRAINS

MOROCCAN CHICKPEA CASSEROLE

This is an easy, self-contained dish that's full of flavor. Just serve it with a leafy salad or a Middle Eastern Carrot Salad (*see page 66*).

serves 4

2 onions, minced
2 tablespoons olive oil
2 teaspoons cumin seeds
2 teaspoons coriander seeds, lightly crushed
4 garlic cloves, chopped
2 eggplant, cut into chunks
1 red chili pepper
1 teaspoon saffron strands
1 teaspoon salt
4 cups (425 g) canned chickpeas
½ cup (175 g) basmati rice
½ cup (115 g) large green olives
1 thin-skinned lemon, sliced
2½ cups (600 ml) vegetable broth
handful of fresh coriander (cilantro), roughly chopped

Sauté the onions in the oil in a large skillet for 5 minutes. Stir in the cumin and coriander seeds, the garlic, eggplant, chili pepper, saffron, and salt, and leave to cook for a couple of minutes while you drain the chickpeas into a sieve and rinse under cold running water (to get rid of excess salt).

Add the chickpeas to the skillet along with the rice, olives, and lemon slices, then pour the broth into the mixture. Bring to the boil, cover, and cook gently for 20 minutes. Fork the chopped coriander through the mixture and serve.

IRON-RICH BREAKFAST MIX

I owe this, and some of the iron-boosting ideas on page 19, to Peter Cox author of the *Encyclopedia of Vegetarian Living* (see *page 189*). Mix together 1½ tablespoons (25 g) each of sesame seeds and sunflower seeds, and 2 tablespoons (50 g) each of pistachio nuts, pumpkin seeds (pepitas), and rolled (old-fashioned) oats. Stir in 1 tablespoon blackstrap molasses and enough fruit juice to cover, and leave to soak. Serve with fresh fruit to taste. This provides a hefty 25 mg of iron; you could eat it in two or more portions throughout the day.

BREAKFAST SMOOTHIE

A smoothie is simply a slightly thickened "shake" that you can whip up in no time if you've got a blender or food processor, and to which you can add all kinds of nutritious ingredients. I like to use soy milk, rice milk, or almond milk as the base, then add any of the following: a small peeled banana or avocado, a handful of washed blueberries or strawberries, a tablespoon or two of ground almonds—which add extra iron, as does a tablespoon of molasses—two or three teaspoonfuls of wheat germ or oat germ, a dash of vanilla extract, or a spoonful of apple juice concentrate for sweetness.

MUESLI OR GRANOLA

There are many muesli and granola mixes on the market, and which one you choose—or whether you make your own—is really a question of taste. I'd go for an organic mix, without added sugar, although some good ones have a little sweetening from added apple juice and/or a touch of honey. One of my favorites contains jumbo oats, crunchy oat bran flakes, roasted hazelnuts, pumpkin seeds, sesame seeds, and dried fruits—blueberries, cranberries, nectarines, and strawberries. You could make something similar by combining these ingredients yourself. Spread out the grains, nuts, and seeds on a cookie sheet and toast in a moderate oven for 15–20 minutes, or until they smell fragrant, stirring them a few times. Cool, then mix with the dried fruits. I would also add some "popped" amaranth or quinoa (see *page 110*) for wonderful balanced protein, and, just before serving, top with a tablespoon of freshly ground golden flaxseeds for their omega-3 oils.

TOFU SCRAMBLE

Mash the drained contents of 2 cup or an 8-ounce (250-g) package of firm or silken tofu until it looks like scrambled eggs. Heat 1 tablespoon of canola oil in a saucepan, add the mashed tofu, half a teaspoon of turmeric for color, 1 tablespoon of soy sauce, and some salt and freshly ground black pepper. Stir until hot, then serve as it is, or on hot toast. You could sauté a chopped onion, garlic, tomatoes, or sliced mushrooms in the oil before adding the tofu, for extra interest.

OAT, MILLET, OR OTHER GRAIN MUSH

Measure 1 cup rolled oats, flaked millet, or another grain, such as flaked rice, barley, or quinoa (or a mixture of these) into a saucepan and add 1 cup water and 1 cup milk or soy milk. Stir over the heat for a few minutes until thick and creamy. Serve as it is or topped with flaked almonds, raisins, soaked dried fruits, chopped fresh fruits, a swirl of apple juice concentrate, a scattering of ground flaxseeds, some sesame seeds, or gomashio (see page 158).

SOY YOGURT

There is a wonderful thick and creamy unsweetened soy yogurt that I first discovered in France and may now be available from your local health food store (see page 188). I love to eat it chilled, straight from the pot, or with some oat bran stirred in. You might also try it swirled with maple syrup or maple sugar, with chopped dried, fresh, or soaked fruits, or with toasted nuts and seeds. If you want to make your own soy yogurt, use an electric yogurt maker, following the manufacturer's instructions, using a little live cows' or goats' milk yogurt to start it off, then saving a little soy yogurt from each batch to start the next. Alternatively, do as I do. Sterilize three 2-cup (450-g) jelly jars or Mason jars by heating them in a cool oven for 10 minutes or so. Cool, then put 1 teaspoon of live yogurt into each and top up with soy milk that feels comfortably hot to your finger. Screw down the lids, wrap in a warm towel or blanket, and put in a warm place, such as a warm radiator in winter, or a sheltered stoop, out of the sun, in summer, for about 8 hours or until set.

VEGETARIAN SUSHI

These are a quite a lot of trouble to make, but fun nonetheless. Once you get into the swing of it they're much quicker to roll up than you'd think. If you're making these for a party, it's best to include the wasabi—Japanese ground green horseradish—in the rolls, along with a little pickled ginger and a sprinkle of dipping sauce, but if you're making them for a small number of people, it's more fun for each guest to have their own little dollop of wasabi, a small pile of pink pickled ginger furls, and a tiny bowl of dipping sauce. You can buy all these at an oriental grocery store, and even in some supermarkets in ethnic neighborhoods. Wasabi comes ready-made in a tube or you can buy the powder, which takes about 5 seconds to mix with water at home. While you're in the store, buy one of the small woven mats they sell for rolling the sushi on—but don't worry if you haven't got one, just improvise with a square of thick plastic.

makes 40–48

1 cup (250 g) Japanese
  sticky rice
2 tablespoons rice vinegar
2 tablespoons mirin
1 teaspoon salt
5–6 sheets of nori
  seaweed, ready toasted

FOR THE FILLING
4–6 asparagus spears,
  not too thick
1 red bell pepper, broiled,
  cooled, and skinned
1 yellow bell pepper,
  broiled, cooled, and
  skinned
1 small avocado
small piece of plain or
  smoked tofu

FOR THE DIP
3 tablespoons soy sauce
3 tablespoons mirin
1 teaspoon grated fresh
  ginger
½ teaspoon sesame seeds

TO SERVE
wasabi
Japanese pickled ginger

Put the rice into a saucepan with 2½ cups (600 ml) water. Bring to the boil, cover, reduce the heat, and leave to cook very gently for 15 minutes. Stir in the vinegar, mirin, and salt. Cover the pan and leave to cool.

Next, prepare the fillings. You need long strips, about the size of the asparagus spears, so cut your bell peppers, avocado, and tofu accordingly. You'll only need a few strips of each.

continued overleaf

Now for the fun. Put your sushi mat or a piece of plastic, measuring around 8½ × 9½ inches (22 × 24 cm) in front of you. Have beside you a little bowl of cold water for moistening your fingers, as well as the rice and other ingredients.

Place a sheet of nori on the mat and spoon about 3 tablespoons of sticky rice on top. Using your fingers, spread it over the nori, leaving ½ inch (1 cm) clear all round. Don't worry if there are some gaps. Take one of your fillings—the asparagus spears are easy to start with—and lay them on top of the rice along the end nearest to you, about ½ inch (1 cm) in from the edge of the rice.

Then, starting with the end nearest to you, pull the edge of the nori and the rice up against the asparagus spears and then keep rolling it, firmly, like a jellyroll, using the mat or plastic to help you. When you're done, give it one more press to hold it all together, and put it onto a plate.

Continue in the same way, using the other fillings, on their own or a couple at a time, until you've used all the rice and have 5 or 6 rolls. Chill them for at least 30 minutes, then, using a sharp serrated knife, cut each roll into about 8 pieces, discarding the ends.

To make the dipping sauce, just mix everything together and put into a small bowl or bowls. Serve the sushi with the dipping sauce, wasabi, and pickled ginger.

SUSHI HANDROLLS Serve small squares of nori and all the ingredients in little bowls and let people roll their own nori into cone shapes and fill them with sushi rice and their chosen fillings. Serve with the wasabi, pickled ginger, dipping sauce, and sesame seeds.

SEAWEEDS, SEA VEGETABLES Like many of the more unusual ingredients in this book, seaweed (algae) is something that really grows on you! It contains numerous nutrients (see page 11); some seaweeds even contain the elusive long-chain omega-3 fatty acids. Flavorwise, I think seaweed is exquisite. Buy some, try it, and see. Flat sheets of toasted nori are easy to use—just snip shreds over the top of steamed or stir-fried vegetables, salads or grain dishes, or make them into sushi rolls or cones (see above). Hijiki and arame are particular favorites of mine. Both need rinsing, then simmering in a little water for a few minutes until they're tender. Don't let the potent smell of the sea from the raw seaweed put you off; once they're cooked, they don't taste or smell strong. You'll find recipes using them on pages 158 and 160; I wish there had been room for more. I didn't have space, either, for recipes using wakame or dulse, but you prepare and use them in the same way, and they're equally delicious. Kombu is useful because it helps to tenderize beans and gives flavor to grains—just rinse a piece to remove excess salt and add it to the pot. Remove after cooking and discard, though some addicts have been known to cut it up and eat it, maybe sprinkled with a little rice vinegar and soy sauce. Dulse used to be a popular snack, sold at fairgrounds, in northern Ireland.

RISOTTO WITH ROSEMARY AND LEMON

This simple risotto needs very few ingredients yet tastes divine. You can even make a particularly delicious vegan version (*see below*).

serves 4

1 tablespoon olive oil
1 celery heart, finely chopped
1 bunch of green onions (scallions), chopped
2 large garlic cloves, crushed
1¾ cups (400 g) arborio or risotto rice
2 glasses vermouth or dry white wine
5 cups (1.2 liters) vegetable broth
grated rind of 1 lemon
1 tablespoon rosemary, chopped
4 tablespoons (2 oz) butter
½ cup (115 g) grated Parmesan cheese

Heat the olive oil in a large saucepan, add the celery and green onions (scallions). Stir, then add the garlic and rice. Stir again, then pour in the vermouth or wine, and let it bubble away as you stir.

Now add a ladleful of the broth, still stirring. When it has been absorbed, add another ladleful and continue until the rice is tender—about 25 minutes. Stir in the grated lemon rind, rosemary, butter, and Parmesan. Cover with a folded cloth and leave for a minute or two for the flavorings to melt creamily into the rice, then stir with a fork, and serve.

I like this with a leaf salad containing some peppery leaves such as arugula or cress.

For a vegan version, leave out the Parmesan and butter and instead stir in another couple of tablespoons of olive oil and ½ cup (120 ml) soy milk (see *page 169*) into the risotto for a very silky, yummy dish.

WARM BEET AND QUINOA TABBOULEH

I love raw grated beets and one day I served them with some hot cooked quinoa. They mixed together on my plate and that was enough to set me off. Several versions later, this one, with the sweetness of the onion, is everyone's favorite, though for a simpler version you could leave out the onion and serve it as it is, or maybe with a few raisins stirred in.

serves 4

½ cup (115 g) quinoa
2 tablespoons olive oil
2 large red onions, finely sliced
2 tablespoons balsamic vinegar
2 tablespoons freshly squeezed lemon juice
2 small raw beets, grated (about 1 cup/200 g)
handful of flat-leaf parsley, coarsely chopped, plus extra to serve
salt and freshly ground black pepper
red Swiss chard leaves or other green salad leaves, to serve

Put the quinoa in a sieve and rinse thoroughly under cold running water, then put into a saucepan with 1¼ cups (300 ml) water and bring to the boil. Cover and leave to cook slowly for 18 minutes. Remove from the heat and leave to stand, still covered, for 5 minutes.

Meanwhile, warm the olive oil in a deep, wide saucepan, add the onions, stir to coat with the oil, then cover and leave to cook gently for 10 minutes, or until very tender.

Stir the balsamic vinegar into the onions, let it bubble, then remove from the heat. Add the quinoa, lemon juice, beets, parsley, and plenty of salt and freshly ground black pepper to taste. Scatter a little more parsley over the top and serve with red Swiss chard leaves.

MILLET WITH PEPPERY LEAVES AND AVOCADO

"Peppery leaves" can include watercress, garden cress, chia, peppergrass, and arugula, along with radicchio, and a few oakleaf lettuce leaves.

serves 4 as a side-dish or appetizer, 2 as an entrée

I cup (225 g) millet
salt
a few pine nuts
I ripe avocado
2 cups (85 g) arugula, watercress, or other leaves
grated rind and juice of I lemon or lime
I–2 tablespoons olive oil
freshly ground black pepper

Put the millet into a sieve and rinse under cold running water, then tip into a saucepan, and stir over moderate heat for 3–4 minutes or until the millet has dried and is beginning to smell toasted.

Pour 2½ cups (600 ml) boiling water into the millet. Be prepared for the mixture to seethe and steam as the water is added—the steam can be very hot so protect your hands if necessary. Add ½ teaspoon salt, cover the pan, and leave to cook gently for 15 minutes.

Remove the pan from the heat and leave to stand for 5 minutes—the millet will become dry and fluffy.

Meanwhile, toast the pine nuts. Spread them out on a dry cookie sheet and put under a hot broiler for a minute or so. As soon as they turn golden (watch them carefully), remove them from the broiler and tip into a cold dish so they don't continue cooking and burn.

Peel and slice the avocado. Arrange the salad leaves around the sides of a bowl or serving dish. Spoon the millet into the center and scatter the avocado over the top. Sprinkle the lemon or lime juice and olive oil over the dish, sprinkle with salt, the lemon, or lime rind and the toasted pine nuts, grind some pepper over the dish, and serve.

BAKED BROWN RICE AND MUSHROOMS

I'm tempted to call this a risotto, but to be honest, it hasn't quite got the creamy texture of a real risotto. It is, however, a great dish in its own right, full of rich flavors and chewy textures, and a joy to make because the oven does all the work. For best results, use the type of rice specified (see *page 111*).

serves 4

½-ounce (15-g) package or 1 tablespoon dried porcini mushrooms
1 onion, minced
2 tablespoons olive oil
4 garlic cloves, minced
4 cups (500 g) Portobello mushrooms, sliced
350 g (12 oz) Italian organic short-grain brown rice
⅔ cup (150 ml) dry vermouth or dry sherry
salt and freshly ground black pepper
minced parsley and grated or flaked Parmesan cheese, to serve (optional)

Preheat the oven to 300°F (150°C). Put a large, deep pot or Dutch oven (big enough to hold the rice, the liquid, and all the other ingredients) in the oven to heat up.

Put the dried mushrooms into a jug and top up with 2½ cups (600 ml) boiling water. Set aside.

Gently sauté the onion in the olive oil in a large saucepan for 10 minutes or until soft. Stir in the garlic and Portobello mushrooms and cook, uncovered, for 10 minutes or until the mushrooms are tender.

Stir in the rice, then pour in the vermouth or sherry and stir again until all the liquid has bubbled away.

Add the dried mushrooms and all their liquid, plus another 3 cups (750 ml) hot water, 2 teaspoons of salt and a good grinding of black pepper. Bring to the boil, then transfer everything to the pot or Dutch oven and place, uncovered, in the oven. Bake for 1 hour, stirring from time to time, then serve at once with the parsley and Parmesan, if using.

OATCAKES

Why bother to make oatcakes? Because these are unlike any you can buy—thin, crisp and, I think, utterly delicious. But you must use the right oatmeal, it should be very fine, almost like flour. Eat them with soft goat cheese or any of the dips on pages 86 and 87. I particularly like them with Light and Creamy Hummus. Or serve them for breakfast with butter and orange marmalade for a real treat.

makes 16

1⅓ cups (140 g) fine oatmeal, plus extra for rolling out
½ teaspoon salt
1 teaspoon olive oil

Preheat the oven to 350°F (180°C).

Put the oatmeal into a bowl. Mix the salt and olive oil with ½ cup (125 ml) boiling water, stir to dissolve the salt, then pour the liquid over the oatmeal and mix. Leave for a few minutes to allow the oatmeal to swell, then divide the mixture in half, and form each half into a ball.

Roll out each ball of dough into a circle, using plenty of oatmeal on your board to prevent sticking, then cut into 8 equal slices, like a cake.

Take each slice and roll it from edge to edge, making it as thin as you can. Place on a cookie sheet—they can be close together as they won't spread—and bake for 10 minutes, or until the top is set, then turn them over and bake for a further 5 minutes, to cook the other side.

Cool on a wire rack, then serve. Store any that are left over in an airtight container.

BUCKWHEAT WITH LEMON AND HERBS

Buckwheat is almost as quick to prepare as couscous and bulgur wheat but much healthier and far more interesting. Prepared simply, as here, it makes a superb accompaniment to all kinds of vegetable dishes—roasted, stir-fried, etc.—or it can be turned into the focus of a meal by adding some more substantial ingredients, such as cubes of feta cheese, marinated tofu, or cashew nuts. I recommend organic, untoasted buckwheat—it's far tastier than the other types.

serves 4

1 cup (250 g) organic, untoasted buckwheat
1 tablespoon olive oil
long strands of rind from 1 lemon
juice of 1 lemon
4 heaping tablespoons minced flat-leaf parsley
4 heaping tablespoons minced chives
6 green onions (scallions), cut into shreds
salt and freshly ground black pepper

Rinse the buckwheat in a sieve under cold running water, then put it into a dry saucepan, and cook over a moderate heat for about 5 minutes, stirring from time to time, until it smells fragrantly toasted, and looks a little more golden.

Pour 2½ cups (600 ml) boiling water into the saucepan, standing well back to avoid being scalded from the cloud of steam that will rise. Cover the pan and leave for 15 minutes, off the heat, for an al dente result (which I prefer) or over a gentle heat if you want it softer. I told you it was as easy as couscous!

Using a fork, stir the olive oil, lemon rind and juice, parsley, chives, and green onions (scallions) into the buckwheat. Season with salt and pepper and serve.

MILLET AND CAULIFLOWER MASH

When you purée cooked millet and cauliflower together they look like mashed potatoes, and are a favorite in macrobiotic diets in which potatoes are generally avoided. I like this mixture because it's a different way of serving a grain and has a lower GI rating than mashed potatoes. It goes with anything that's good with mashed potatoes, such as Broiled Seitan with Onions (see *page 154*), or any bean dish. If there's any left over, form it into little patties, coat with flour (I use barley or millet flour) and sauté in olive oil, until crisp and golden, for potato-style cakes.

serves 4–6

I cup (225 g) millet
I medium cauliflower (weighing about I pound/450 g after trimming)
2 tablespoons olive oil
2 garlic cloves, crushed
I tablespoon Dijon mustard
4–6 tablespoons minced parsley
2 green onions (scallions), chopped
salt and freshly ground black pepper

Put the millet into a dry skillet and set over a medium heat for about 4 minutes, stirring often, until it smells fragrantly toasted. Standing back, because it will sizzle, pour in 3¾ cups (850 ml) water, cover, and leave to cook for 15 minutes. It will be pale, fluffy, and all the water will have been absorbed.

Meanwhile, divide the cauliflower into florets and cook in I inch (2.5 cm) boiling water in a pan, covered, until tender. This should take about 6–7 minutes, depending on the size of the pieces. Drain, saving the water.

Purée the cauliflower and millet in a food processor, adding a little of the cauliflower water if necessary, to make a creamy mixture, then add the olive oil, garlic, mustard, parsley, green onions (scallions), and salt and pepper to taste, then blend again briefly.

KHITCHARI

Comforting mixtures of lentils and rice are found in many countries; in the Middle East it's known as *m'jadra*, and in India it's known as khitchari. It is used as a basic healing and cleansing food in Ayurvedic medicine and is also considered nourishing food for children. It's wonderful when you're feeling a bit below par—soothing and reviving at the same time, the spicing delicate and, according to Ayurvedic principles, suitable for every *dosha*, or in other words, for everyone. White basmati rice is used in preference to any other because it is considered to be the most digestible. But don't wait until you're feeling unwell to try it; make it soon. I hope you'll love it as much as I do.

serves 4

½ cup (115 g) white basmati rice
4 tablespoons (2 oz) split mung beans (or use yellow split peas
  or split red lentils)
1 tablespoon pure ghee, clarified butter, or oil
½ teaspoon fennel seeds
½ teaspoon cumin seeds or powdered cumin
½ teaspoon ground coriander
½ teaspoon ground turmeric

Wash the rice and beans together in cold water.

Heat the ghee, butter, or oil in a pan and add the fennel seeds and the cumin, if using seeds. Stir for a minute over the heat, then add the rest of the spices, including the cumin, if using powder, and the rice and beans, and stir to coat with the oil and spices.

Pour in enough boiling water to cover the rice and beans by 2 inches (5 cm). Bring back to the boil and leave to simmer gently, stirring occasionally and making sure the mixture doesn't stick to the pan. Add more water if necessary. The khitchari is cooked when the rice and beans are both soft and most of the liquid has been absorbed. This is quite a soft dish, and not too dry.

SAFFRON RISOTTO CAKE WITH RED BELL PEPPERS

This can be made in advance and kept in the refrigerator or freezer ready for cooking.

serves 6

butter or margarine, for greasing
2 tablespoons dry bread crumbs
2 red bell peppers, seeded and halved
2 tablespoons olive oil
I onion, peeled and chopped
2 large garlic cloves, crushed
1¾ cups (400 g) short-grain or risotto rice
I package or I teaspoon saffron threads
⅔ cup (150 ml) vermouth or white wine
I teaspoon vegetable bouillon powder
½ cup (115 g) freshly grated Parmesan cheese (optional)
salt and freshly ground black pepper
some red bell pepper strips and green leaves, e.g., flat-leaf parsley, to serve

Preheat the oven to 350°F (180°C). Line the base of a 2-pound (900-g) loaf pan with a strip of nonstick baking paper, then grease with butter or margarine and sprinkle with bread crumbs.

Broil the peppers, cut-side down, for about 10 minutes, or until tender and black in places. Leave to cool.

Heat the olive oil in a large saucepan and add the onion. Stir, then cover and cook for 7 minutes. Add the garlic, rice, and saffron. Stir well, then add the vermouth or wine and let it bubble away as you stir.

Measure 3¾ cups (850 ml) boiling water into a pan, add the bouillon powder, and keep the water very gently simmering. Add a ladleful to the rice, while stirring. When this has been absorbed, add another ladleful and continue until all the liquid has been added and the rice is tender—about 25 minutes. Stir in the Parmesan, if using. Cover the pan with a cloth. Leave for 5 minutes to settle, then season with salt and pepper to taste.

Skin the bell peppers—you don't need to be too particular about this; just remove the black bits that will come away easily.

Put a third of the rice mixture into the loaf pan, then place two pepper halves on top. Spoon another third of the rice on top, followed by two more pepper halves, then the rest of the rice. Press down well.

Cover the pan with foil and bake for 30–40 minutes. Remove from the oven and let it stand for 3–4 minutes, then slip a knife round the sides and unmold onto a warmed serving platter. Garnish with pieces of red bell pepper and green leaves. To serve, cut into thick slices with a sharp knife. This must be done carefully if the cake is to be eaten warm.

BARLEY AND MUSHROOM RISOTTO

Barley is a plump, sweet grain that needn't be confined to stews and soups. It can be quite glamorous if you make it into a risotto.
I love to use juicy Portobello mushrooms and, to start the risotto off, whisky seems just right (cheap whisky, of course, nothing fancy).

serves 4

½-ounce (15-g) package or 1 tablespoon dried porcini mushrooms
2 teaspoons vegetable bouillon powder
1 onion, minced
2 sticks celery, finely chopped
2 tablespoons olive oil
4 garlic cloves, minced
5 cups (500 g) Portobello mushrooms, sliced
1½ cups (350 g) organic pearl barley
⅓ cup (100 ml) whiskey
2–4 tablespoons (25–50 g) butter (optional)
salt and freshly ground black pepper
Grated or flaked Parmesan cheese, to serve (optional)

Put the dried porcini into a saucepan with 5 cups (1.2 liters) water and the bouillon powder. Bring to the boil, then set aside.

Sauté the onion and celery in the oil for 5 minutes, then add the garlic, mushrooms, and barley and stir so that they become glossy with oil.

Add the whiskey and when it has sizzled away, stir in a ladleful of the porcini water. Keep stirring, and when the liquid has boiled away again, add another ladleful. Continue in this way until all the water, and the porcini mushrooms in it, have been added and the barley is soft and creamy. This will take about 30–35 minutes and you can be more relaxed about the stirring as the cooking progresses.

Remove the pan from the heat, stir in the butter, if using, and season to taste. Then leave the pan, covered, to stand for 10 minutes. Serve with grated or flaked Parmesan, if using.

LEMON RICE

This pretty, primrose yellow rice is easy to make and goes with many spicy dishes.

serves 4 as an accompaniment

I teaspoon turmeric
I cup (250 g) basmati rice
salt and freshly ground black pepper
grated rind and juice of I lemon

Bring 4 cups (1 liter) water to the boil in a saucepan, stir in the turmeric, and add the rice. Boil, uncovered, for 6–7 minutes, or until the grain is tender but still has a little resistance.

Drain the rice into a sieve, then return it to the saucepan with salt and pepper to taste.

Using a fork, gently stir in the lemon rind and juice. As you do so, the rice will change from a dull gold to an uplifting, bright, primrose yellow. Reheat gently and serve.

LEMON RICE WITH WILD RICE Instead of plain white basmati or other long-grain rice, buy a package of mixed long-grain or Carolina and wild rice, and use that instead—the dark strands of wild rice look pretty against the golden rice, and taste good, too.

TOFU, TEMPEH, AND SEITAN

TOFU, TEMPEH, AND SEITAN ARE THE ORIGINAL VEGETARIAN PROTEIN FOODS, AND HAVE BEEN USED IN CHINA AND JAPAN FOR CENTURIES. THEY'RE MADE FROM NATURAL INGREDIENTS—SOY, IN THE CASE OF TOFU AND TEMPEH, WHEAT GLUTEN FOR SEITAN—AND IF, LIKE ME, YOU BUY THEM IN THEIR SIMPLE, TRADITIONAL FORM (AS OPPOSED TO "BACON-FLAVORED," ETC.), THEY MAKE A WONDERFUL BASE FOR ALL KINDS OF MEALS. THEY'RE ALL RICH IN PROTEIN AND LOW IN FAT AND CARBOHYDRATES, AND ARE VERY HEALTH-GIVING, AS WELL AS BEING EASY TO USE AND DELICIOUS.

NATURAL PROTEIN FOODS

Tofu

Tofu is made by first soaking, then puréeing, gently simmering, and straining soybeans to make soy milk. This is then mixed with an acidic ingredient such as calcium chloride, that makes it separate into curds and whey. The curds are strained into a mold and pressed, and the result is tofu. It's a natural process that you could undertake at home, and indeed I have done so. These days, however, I prefer to buy my tofu from the refrigerated section of a good health food store. It keeps well in its package, which will contain some water, for several days in the refrigerator. The various brands have slightly different flavors and textures, so experiment with a few to find the one you prefer. You can buy both firm and silken tofu. I use firm for everything, but silken is good for creamy dips, dressings, and whips. My favorites are listed on page 189. You can get various "flavored" tofus and tofu-based foods; I much prefer plain, natural tofu—or, in a pinch, the smoked variety, for some dishes—because it's so versatile, and it's easy to add your own flavorings. Tofu is wonderful marinated in garlic, ginger, soy sauce, and mirin (see *Griddled Tofu with Chili, Bok Choy, and Ginger on page 142*).

Tempeh

Tempeh (pronounced "tem-pay") is made from cooked soybeans that have been fermented. It's been made like this in Indonesia for centuries and is a traditional food throughout the country. It's very digestible so it is a useful high-protein, low-fat, nutritious food for the very young and the elderly. You could make it at home but it's much easier to buy it; it looks like a café-au-lait-colored slab with a lumpy texture and is to be found in the refrigerated section of the same health food stores that sell good-quality tofu. Choose a pale one without black flecks in it: these are edible but they tend to give it a stronger flavor.

The simplest way to prepare tempeh is to slice it, brush it with a little canola oil, and broil it, then sprinkle with soy sauce or with a spicy sweet pickles. I like to serve watercress with it.

Seitan

Seitan (pronounced "say-tan") is another protein ingredient that's so natural and traditional that you could easily make it at home if you wanted to. The process is a little like making a sourdough. You make a dough from high-gluten or all-purpose flour and water, knead it, then leave it to soak in water for a while. After that, you start gently pressing and rinsing it, and as you do so a white liquid comes out—this is the starch. You keep going until the water runs clear and the lump of "dough" becomes quite bouncy and springy: that's your seitan. You then simmer it in flavored broth, drain it, and use as required.

You can also buy seitan in the same places that sell good tofu and tempeh. You might have to hunt among all the "flavored" varieties and mock meats for a natural, unflavored one—it looks like a rather unappetizing brown lump in a plastic pack. It's very high in protein and virtually fat free.

To cook seitan, simply drain it, pat dry on paper towels, slice with a sharp knife—I like it cut quite thin—then either toss in a little canola oil and broil or sauté. I like it quite crisp, but stop cooking when it's as you want it. It's undeniably chewy, which I love because it adds a texture to vegetarian cooking.

WARM SMOKY TOFU AND BROCCOLI SALAD

I love this combination of crisp, smoky tofu and tender broccoli, with its sweet-and-sour ginger dressing. And it's so quick and easy to make.

serves 2 for an entrée

- 1 pound (450 g) broccoli
- 1 cup (250 g) smoked tofu
- vegetable oil
- 1 tablespoon soy sauce
- 1 tablespoon toasted sesame oil
- 1 tablespoon mirin
- 1 tablespoon rice vinegar
- 1 teaspoon grated ginger
- 1 garlic clove, crushed

Divide the broccoli into florets, cutting larger ones in half so they're all roughly the same size. In a saucepan, bring 1 inch (2.5 cm) of water to the boil. Add the broccoli, cover, and cook for about 4 minutes, or until the broccoli is just tender to the point of a knife.

Meanwhile drain the tofu, pat dry on paper towels, and cut into very thin slices. Pour about 3 tablespoons of oil into a skillet, heat, and add a single layer of tofu. Sauté until the tofu is crisp and brown on one side, then flip the pieces over. When they're done, drain on paper towels. You will probably have to cook the tofu in several batches.

Drain the broccoli, then return it to the pan with the soy sauce, sesame oil, mirin, rice vinegar, grated ginger, and garlic. Toss lightly, then stir in the crisp tofu, and serve.

VINEGARS I find the most useful are rice vinegar, for oriental dishes, and because it's so (naturally) sweet and light that you can use more than the usual proportions in dressings and so need less oil; balsamic vinegar—the best I can afford—for its sweetness; red wine vinegar, although I find I use this a lot less than I used to because I'm so fond of rice vinegar, and also because I've gone back to my vegetarian roots and taken to using organic apple cider vinegar again. The latter is light, sweet, and fruity, and is also said to alkalize the system and have all kinds of therapeutic properties, including staving off or easing arthritis.

GRIDDLED TOFU WITH CHILI PEPPER, BOK CHOY, AND GINGER

Tofu can taste superb—yes, it really can. It all starts, as with most cooking, with your choice of ingredients. Buy the right type of tofu (see page 189), cook it with lively flavorings, and you've got a dish anyone would enjoy. Using a griddle or griddle pan gives the tofu attractive stripes, but if you haven't got one, cut the tofu into cubes and sauté it in a skillet with the mushrooms. It will taste just as good.

serves 2

1 cup (250-g block) of organic, firm tofu
2 large garlic cloves, crushed
1 tablespoon grated fresh ginger
1–2 tablespoons soy sauce, plus a little extra for serving
1 tablespoon mirin
2 × 7-ounce (200-g) packages bok choy
2 tablespoons canola oil
2 cups (250 g) fresh shiitake or Portobello mushrooms, washed and sliced
½ a mild red chili pepper, seeded and chopped
2 small green onions (scallions), sliced
salt and freshly ground black pepper
1–2 teaspoons dark sesame oil (optional)
½–1 teaspoon toasted sesame seeds (see page 60)

Drain the tofu, then cut it crosswise into rectangles around ¼ inch (5 mm) thick. Cut these into triangles and place in a shallow dish. Mix together half the garlic, half the ginger, the soy sauce, and mirin and pour the liquid over the tofu, making sure all the pieces are coated. Set aside.

Wash and slice the bok choy. Heat 1 tablespoon of the oil in a wok or large saucepan and add the mushrooms, bok choy, chili pepper, green onions (scallions), and the remaining garlic and ginger. Stir-fry for about 6 minutes, or until the bok choy is tender but still crisp.

Meanwhile, brush the griddle pan with the remaining oil and heat it. Pick up a piece of tofu, letting the excess liquid run back onto the plate. Place the tofu on the hot griddle pan, then repeat with the rest of the tofu (you may have to do it in more than one batch, depending on the size of your griddle). Cook for 2–3 minutes, until the tofu is sealed and seared and has appetizing brown stripes, then flip the pieces over to cook the other side.

Add any remaining tofu marinade to the bok choy mixture, stir and season with salt, freshly ground black pepper, the sesame oil, if you're using it, and a dash of soy sauce. Serve with the griddled tofu, sprinkled with the sesame seeds.

TOFU AND MUSHROOM SKEWERS

Use two metal skewers, or two wooden ones that have been soaked in cold water for 10 minutes or more, so that they won't burn in the heat. Serve with Quick and Easy Peanut Sauce (*see page 146*) and some Cumin-roasted Sweet Potatoes (*see page 42*).

serves 2

1 cup (250 g) tofu
1 tablespoon soy sauce
1 tablespoon toasted sesame oil
1 tablespoon mirin
1 teaspoon grated ginger
1 garlic clove, crushed
¾ cup (85 g) baby Portobello mushrooms

Drain the tofu, pat dry on paper towels, and cut into cubes—around 10 is ideal. In a shallow dish that will hold the tofu, combine the soy sauce, sesame oil, mirin, ginger, and garlic to make a marinade. Add the tofu and turn to coat it

Wash the mushrooms but don't remove the stalks. Slice them in half, if necessary. Thread a mushroom onto a skewer, followed by a cube of tofu, then another mushroom, and so on—packing them tightly together. When both skewers are crammed full, brush them with the remaining soy sauce mixture. They can wait, sitting in their marinade, for several hours, or you can broil or grill them straight away.

When you're ready, prepare a hot broiler or grill. Put the skewers on a metal sheet under the broiler or on the grill and spoon any extra marinade over them. Cook until they're stickily brown and lightly caramelized and smell fragrant—around 6 minutes under a hot broiler, turning them after around 4 minutes. Serve at once.

QUICK AND EASY PEANUT SAUCE

This is a delicious peanut sauce with a hint of sweetness and a savory undertone. Put 4 tablespoons peanut butter into a bowl and stir in 1 teaspoon honey, apple juice concentrate, or agave syrup (see *page 164*); 1 teaspoon of miso (I use organic whole barley miso); and 2–3 tablespoons of boiling water. You could also add a crushed garlic clove, if you want extra flavor.

TARTAR SAUCE

Pour 5 tablespoons soy milk into a blender or food processor with 2 tablespoons fresh lemon juice, 1 teaspoon Dijon mustard, 1 tablespoon wine vinegar or cider vinegar, a crushed small garlic clove, salt and pepper, and blend briefly. Drizzle 1 scant cup (200 ml) light olive oil through the lid while continuing to process. The mixture should thicken, like mayonnaise. Transfer to a bowl and serve as it is, or stir in 1 tablespoon chopped capers and 1 tablespoon of chopped pickled cucumber.

MADEIRA GRAVY

Heat 2 tablespoons of canola oil in a saucepan. Add 2 tablespoons of whole wheat flour and stir over the heat for a minute or two until nut-brown. Then add a ½-ounce (15-g) package or 1 tablespoon dried porcini mushrooms and 2½ cups (600 ml) water or vegetable broth. Stir over the heat for 2–3 minutes, until thickened, then leave over a gentle heat for 7–10 minutes to cook the flour. Stir in 1 tablespoon soy sauce, 2 tablespoons madeira or sherry, and salt and pepper to taste. Strain before using, reserving the pieces of porcini to use in future cooking, then blend in a food processor until smooth. Alternatively, do as I do and serve the gravy with the porcini still in it.

TAHINI SAUCE

Put 3 tablespoons of light tahini (you may need to stir the jar first, as tahini tends to separate) into a bowl and stir in 1 tablespoon freshly squeezed lemon juice, 2 tablespoons water, and a crushed garlic clove. If you want the sauce a little thinner, simply stir in a little more water.

CRANBERRY SAUCE

Wash 1 cup (250 g) cranberries, discarding any damaged ones. Put the cranberries into a saucepan with 2 tablespoons apple juice concentrate and ¾ cup (175 g) fructose (see page 164) and place over a medium heat. Cook gently for 4–5 minutes, until the juices run and the cranberries soften but don't go mushy. Serve warm or cold.

LIGHT AND CREAMY WHITE SAUCE

Bring just under 2½ cups (600 ml) soy milk to the boil in a saucepan with a bay leaf and a piece of onion. Leave to stand off the heat while you mix 2 tablespoons of arrowroot or kuzu (see page 159) with a little more soy milk in a bowl to make a smooth paste. Then reheat the milk, mix it into the paste, and return it all to the pan. Stir over the heat for a minute or two until thickened, but don't overcook as the sauce will become thin again. If you like, stir in a tablespoon or two of olive oil for extra richness (or a knob of butter, if you prefer), and salt, pepper, and grated nutmeg to taste. Remove the onion and bay leaf before serving. You could also add freshly minced parsley, grated cheese, or a tablespoon or so of nutritional yeast flakes for a "salty" flavor.

BROILED SPICED TOFU WITH PEPPERS

So you think tofu is bland and flavorless? Well, try this. Sambal Oelek is an Indonesian hot pepper sauce that you can get at any supermarket (read the label and check you're getting a vegetarian one). It keeps for ages in the refrigerator. The light coating of arrowroot or gram flour makes the tofu crisp. Serve with basmati rice and a green leaf salad, if you like.

serves 2

1 red bell pepper, seeded and cut into long slices
1 cup (250 g) tofu
4–6 teaspoons Sambal Oelek
4–6 teaspoons gram flour (see page 102)
  or arrowroot (see page 159)
olive oil
parsley, to garnish

Heat the broiler to high. Start with the peppers, because these take longer to cook. Simply put them in a broiler pan and place under the broiler.

Meanwhile, drain the tofu, cut it in half crosswise, then halve each piece. Spread Sambal Oelek all over the cut surfaces of the tofu, then toss the pieces in the gram flour or arrowroot, pressing it in lightly.

Remove the broiler pan from the broiler, lightly oil the area where the tofu will go, then put the tofu on the broiler pan and turn immediately so the top of each piece is oily. Turn the pieces of pepper as necessary, then put everything back under the broiler.

Broil until the tofu is browned on top—around 4 minutes—then turn the pieces over. The other side won't take as long and by then the peppers will be done, too. Serve at once, garnished with the parsley.

As a variation you could sauté the tofu in oil.

QUICK TOFU CURRY WITH PEAS

Quick, easy, and full of flavor and nourishment—what more could you ask of a dish? It's pretty good just on its own, but you could serve it with some plain boiled white or brown basmati rice or some Indian naan bread. My favorite accompaniment is cauliflower or shredded cabbage, cooked until it's barely tender.

serves 4

1 onion, minced
2 tablespoons vegetable oil
2 garlic cloves, minced
2 teaspoons grated fresh ginger
1 teaspoon cumin seeds
½ teaspoon turmeric
1 cup (250 g) tofu
3 tomatoes, roughly chopped
½ cup (115 g) frozen peas
1 tablespoon fresh lemon juice
salt and freshly ground black pepper
a little fresh coriander (cilantro) (optional)

Cook the onion in the oil in a covered pan for 5 minutes or until the onion is beginning to soften. Stir in the garlic, ginger, cumin, and turmeric, and leave to cook for another minute or so.

Meanwhile, deal with the tofu. It needs to be drained, patted dry with paper towels, then cut into cubes. Add the tofu to the spicy mixture in the pan and cook for 5 minutes over moderate heat, so that it becomes golden brown in places, stirring often.

Add the tomatoes and peas. Cook for 3–4 minutes, until the peas have heated through and the tomatoes have softened. Stir in the lemon juice, taste, and season with salt and pepper. Snip some coriander over the top, if using, and serve.

TEMPEH BURGERS

Apart from just cutting it thinly, frying it until crisp, and serving it with a salad or a richly-flavored onion gravy (*see page 154*), this is my favorite way of using tempeh. This recipe makes four burgers, enough for two people, but the quantities can easily be doubled to make enough for four people. I love these burgers with either a sweet sauce, such as Cranberry Sauce (*see page 147*), or with a sharp, creamy Tartar Sauce (*see page 146*).

serves 2

7-ounce (200-g) package tempeh
2 tablespoons vegetable oil
I onion, minced
2 tablespoons (25 g) all-purpose flour
I garlic clove, crushed
⅓ cup (100 ml) soy milk
2 green onions (scallions), chopped
I tablespoon lemon juice
salt and freshly ground black pepper
vegetable oil for frying

FOR THE COATING
2 tablespoons arrowroot or kuzu (*see page 159*)
5 tablespoons dried bread crumbs

Remove the wrapping from the tempeh and put the whole block into a pan with enough water just to cover. Bring to the boil and simmer for 15 minutes, then drain well and mash roughly.

Heat the oil in a saucepan, add the onion, cover, and cook for 7–10 minutes, or until the onion is tender and lightly browned. Stir the flour and garlic in with the onion, cook over a low heat for 5–7 minutes to cook the flour, then pour in the soy milk, and stir to make a thick sauce. Remove from the heat.

Add the tempeh, green onions (scallions), and lemon juice to the onion mixture. Season well with salt and pepper.

For the coating, mix the arrowroot or kuzu with 2–3 tablespoons water to make a liquid paste (the lumps in the kuzu will disappear like magic when you add the water).

Shape the tempeh mixture into four patties, dip each into the paste, then into the bread crumbs, coating all sides.

Heat ½ inch (1 cm) of vegetable oil in a skillet, add the burgers, and fry for 2–3 minutes on each side until browned and crisp. Drain on paper towels and serve at once.

TOFU, TEMPEH, AND SEITAN

SWEET-AND-SOUR SEITAN

This is a quick and easy dish, full of different flavors. The secret is to make sure you sauté the seitan until it's really crisp before you stir-fry the vegetables.

serves 2–3

2 tablespoons vegetable oil
I cup (225 g) seitan, cut into thin strips
I red bell pepper, cut into strips
2 carrots, cut into strips
I fat zucchini, cut into strips
I small pineapple, peeled and cut into strips,
   or 2 cups (450 g) canned pineapple pieces in juice, drained
bunch of green onions (scallions), cut into strips

FOR THE SAUCE
I tablespoon fresh lemon juice
I tablespoon cider vinegar
I tablespoon soy sauce
I tablespoon liquid honey
I tablespoon grated fresh ginger
2 garlic cloves, crushed
salt and freshly ground black pepper

Heat the oil in a large saucepan or wok and fry the seitan until crisp. Remove the seitan from the pan, then add the vegetables and stir-fry for 3–4 minutes, or until the vegetables are still crisp but getting tender.

Meanwhile, mix all the sauce ingredients in a small bowl with some salt and pepper. Pour the sauce into the vegetables, stirring. Add the seitan and cook for a further minute or two, to get everything hot, then serve.

SOY SAUCE The soy sauce I love is tamari, which is traditionally processed and made without chemicals, sugar, or preservatives, and is becoming much more widely available outside health food and whole food stores.

BROILED SEITAN WITH ONIONS

I love this mixture of chewy seitan and sweet broiled onions; you can stop there, or you can go on to make the onions into a glorious rich gravy in which to serve the seitan.

serves 2

1 cup (225 g) seitan
3 teaspoons canola oil
1 cup (225 g) finely sliced onion
1 teaspoon brown sugar, preferably rapadura (see page 164)
1 tablespoon all-purpose flour
2 teaspoons vegetable bouillon powder
1 teaspoon Dijon mustard
1 teaspoon vegetarian Worcestershire sauce
salt and freshly ground black pepper

Heat the broiler. Drain, pat dry, and slice the seitan quite thinly. Sprinkle with 1 teaspoon of the oil, mix with your fingers so all the seitan is coated, then spread it out on one side of a broiler pan.

Sprinkle the sliced onion with another teaspoon of oil and the sugar. Mix thoroughly with your fingers and put on the other side of the broiler pan.

Broil for around 15 minutes, stirring the pieces around from time to time—but don't mix the onion and seitan—until the onion is tender and both are tinged brown. You can mix them together and serve at this stage, if you wish, or keep the seitan warm under the broiler while you make the onions into a gravy.

To make the gravy, heat the remaining teaspoon of oil in a saucepan, add the onions from the broiler, and also add the flour to the pan. Stir over the heat for 1–2 minutes to brown the flour, then stir in 1¾ cups (400 ml) water, the bouillon powder, mustard, and Worcestershire sauce. Simmer for 5 minutes, season to taste, then serve with the seitan, either separately or all mixed together.

VEGETARIAN WORCESTERSHIRE SAUCE This is available for your cooking and your Bloody Marys, but you may have to seek it out. Standard Worcestershire sauce contains anchovy extract—if in doubt, read the label. Vegetarian Worcestershire sauce is also available in the kosher section of supermarkets.

ASIAN-STYLE BRAISED TEMPEH

This is very tasty and nutritious. Serve it with quickly cooked Asian greens, such as bok choy or mustard greens, or with spinach, and some cellophane noodles or boiled basmati rice, for a more substantial meal.

Serves 2

1 cup (225 g) tempeh, quite thinly sliced
2 tablespoons canola oil
1 tablespoon sesame oil
2 garlic cloves, sliced
1 teaspoon grated ginger
2 tablespoons soy sauce
2 tablespoons mirin
2 green onions (scallions), chopped

Sauté the tempeh in the canola oil, turning it over when the first side is crisp and golden brown, then drain on paper towels. You'll probably need to do it in more than one batch.

When the tempeh is all done, discard any remaining oil from the skillet, clean it with some paper towels and add the sesame oil. Heat, then add all the fried tempeh.

Sizzle for a minute, then add the garlic, ginger, soy sauce, and mirin. Stir over the heat for a few more seconds, until the tempeh is bathed in a glossy brown sauce, then remove from the heat, scatter with the green onions (scallions), and serve.

For an extra kick, you could add some chopped red chili pepper to the mixture when you put the tempeh into the sesame oil.

30-MINUTE MEALS TO SERVE COMPANY

Avocado Dip (see *page 87*)

Pappardelle with Eggplant and Artichoke Hearts (see *page 74*)
   or Tagliatelle with Mushrooms and Cream (see *page 73*)

Little Gem, Belgian Endive, and Watercress Salad (see *page 33*)

Honey and Cinnamon-roasted Figs (see *page 170*)

Thai Beancakes with Sweet Red Pepper Sauce (see *page 92*)

Golden Thai Curry (see *page 38*)

Basmati rice

Oranges and Passion Fruit (see page 165)

Light and Creamy Hummus (see *page 86*)

Golden Rice, Avocados, and Wild Mushrooms (see *page 114*)

Green salad

Raspberries and cream

TOFU AND ARAME SALAD

Sometimes I just fancy a clean-tasting salad with an oil-free Japanese dressing and a tang of the sea, and one day when I was in one of those moods, this is the salad I came up with. Arame (*see page 122*) is a sea vegetable which can be found at good health food stores. You also need a really good-quality tofu, tender and delicate, to make this (*see page 189*).

serves 2–4

2 tablespoons (25 g) arame
1 cup (250 g) tofu, drained and blotted on paper towels
1 tablespoon rice vinegar
1 tablespoon soy sauce
few drops of umeboshi plum seasoning (*see below*) or lemon juice
$\frac{1}{2}$–1 fresh, large, mild red chili pepper, seeded and finely chopped
$\frac{3}{4}$ cup (90-g package) fresh watercress

FOR THE SESAME SALT (GOMASHIO)
2 tablespoons sesame seeds
1 teaspoon sea salt

Cover the arame with boiling water, soak for 5 minutes, then drain, rinse, chop, and put into a bowl.

Cut the tofu into $\frac{1}{4}$ inch (5 mm) cubes and put into the bowl with the arame, rice vinegar, soy sauce, umeboshi plum seasoning or lemon juice, and the chili pepper, and stir together.

Heap the tofu mixture up on a serving dish or on individual plates, and arrange the watercress around the edge.

To make the gomashio, put the sesame seeds and salt into a dry saucepan and stir over the heat until the seeds smell and look toasted and start jumping around in the pan. Grind with a pestle in a mortar or in a clean electric coffee mill, and serve with the salad.

UMEBOSHI PLUMS AND SEASONING Umeboshi is a variety of plum that has been pickled in brine. Its sharp, salty sweetness is very pleasant with Japanese dishes, even just plain cooked rice. You can buy umeboshi plums whole, as a paste, or as a bottled liquid seasoning. They're all quite expensive, but a little goes a long way and they keep for months in the refrigerator.

WESTERN-STYLE TEMPEH WITH MUSHROOMS

I like to use soy milk for this—it seems right to use it with a soy product, and it gives an excellent result. In fact I'd be surprised if anyone could tell the difference between soy milk and milk cream, but if you want to use light cream, please feel free, it will work just as well. Serve with a cooked green vegetable like green string beans, or a green salad, and potatoes or cooked rice.

serves 2

2 cups (225 g) Portobello mushrooms, sliced
2 tablespoons olive oil
1 cup (225 g) tempeh, quite thinly sliced
2 garlic cloves, sliced
1 tablespoon arrowroot or kuzu (*see below*)
1 cup (250 ml) soy milk
juice of ½ a lemon
salt and freshly ground black pepper
grated nutmeg
chopped parsley, to serve

Fry the mushrooms in 1 tablespoon of oil in a large sauté pan or wok for 4–5 minutes, or until they're tender, then remove them from the pan.

Heat the remaining oil in the pan and fry the tempeh on both sides until crisp and golden brown. You'll probably need to do this in more than one batch.

Add the mushrooms and garlic to the tempeh and stir-fry until everything is hot.

Mix the arrowroot or kuzu with enough of the soy milk to make a paste. Add the rest of the milk to the tempeh mixture and bring to the boil, then pour in the arrowroot or kuzu paste and stir until thickened.

Add the lemon juice and salt, pepper, and nutmeg to taste, then remove from the heat, scatter with minced parsley and serve.

KUZU AND ARROWROOT These are both thickeners that can be used like cornstarch, but they're healthier because they have a low paste index and aid digestion. Kuzu looks like lumps of white chalk. Arrowroot is made from a root of that name and comes in the form of a white powder. You can buy both at health food stores and some supermarkets. Arrowroot is less expensive than kuzu.

DEEP-FRIED TOFU AND HIJIKI BALLS

A delicious vegetarian taste of the sea that's packed with nutrients. These are great as an appetizer or to serve with drinks, along with the soy and ginger dip. I must say I also like them with the Tartar Sauce on page 146. You'll find more details on buying and using sea vegetables on page 122.

makes 24

2 tablespoons (25 g) hijiki seaweed
1 cup (250-g package) of tofu, drained and blotted on paper towels
2 tablespoons (50 g) grated carrot or turnip
1 garlic clove, crushed
2 teaspoons grated fresh ginger
salt and freshly ground black pepper
3 tablespoons sesame seeds
vegetable oil

FOR THE DIP
2 tablespoons soy sauce
1 tablespoon mirin
1 teaspoon grated raw ginger

Cover the hijiki with boiling water and soak for 10 minutes. Then drain, cover with fresh water, and simmer for 20 minutes, or until tender. Drain and pat dry with paper towels.

Break up the tofu roughly and put it into a food processor with the hijiki, carrot or turnip, garlic, and ginger, and blend until it becomes a smooth and compact lump. Alternatively, chop the hijiki fairly finely, then mash it with the tofu and other ingredients. Season to taste.

Form the tofu mixture into walnut-sized balls and roll them in the sesame seeds. Make the dip by mixing together the soy sauce, mirin, and ginger.

Fill a saucepan about a third full with vegetable oil and heat. When the oil is hot enough—it's ready when you throw in a sesame seed and it immediately rises to the top and starts to brown—add some of the tofu balls and fry for 3–4 minutes until they're golden brown and crisp. Drain on paper towels and repeat until they're all done. Serve with the dip.

FRUITS, SUGAR, AND SPICE

IF, LIKE ME, YOU'RE NOT KEEN ON USING DAIRY PRODUCE —FOR HEALTH OR ANIMAL WELFARE REASONS—AND YOU ALSO HAVE RESERVATIONS ABOUT FLOUR AND SUGAR BECAUSE OF THEIR HIGH GLYCEMIC INDEX RATING (*SEE PAGE* 9), THEN WHAT IS LEFT FOR SWEET TREATS? A SURPRISING AMOUNT, ACTUALLY, AS I HOPE THIS SECTION OF THE BOOK SHOWS. LUSCIOUS FRUITS, CAKES MADE FROM GROUND ALMONDS, OATS, RICE AND BARLEY FLOURS, AND LOW GLYCEMIC SWEETENERS, AS WELL AS GORGEOUS CREAMS AND TOPPINGS MADE FROM COCONUT AND SOY CREAMER.

SOME HEALTHY SWEETENERS

Agave syrup
When a liquid sweetener can be used, I like agave syrup. It has a low GI rating and is excellent (though a little expensive) for everyday use.

Apple juice concentrate, brown rice syrup, maple syrup
These are my second choices of liquid sweetener. You can buy them from good health food stores. Be sure that the apple juice concentrate and maple syrup are organic, to ensure they are pesticide free. Brown rice syrup is a mild and delicate sweetener, high in complex carbohydrates and with a low GI rating.

Fructose
Instead of superfine sugar you can use fructose, which you can buy in some supermarkets. It behaves in much the same way as far as cooking is concerned (except that it doesn't become crisp, so it's no good for cookies or meringues), and tastes the same too, but has a very low GI rating. I use this for delicate cooking, although it is quite a refined product so it is probably not as healthy an option as rapadura sugar, agave syrup, rice syrup, or apple juice concentrate.

Honey
Although honey has a high GI rating, it has certain therapeutic properties, which make it a special case. Buy a "raw" honey from a health food store, use it sparingly, and don't heat it, because that destroys the benefits. Honey isn't included in a vegan diet.

Molasses
This thick, sticky black syrup is what is taken out of the cane when it's processed to make white sugar. It's full of iron and other minerals, such as potassium, and has a low GI rating, but its strong flavor rather restricts its use.

Rapadura sugar
This product retains all the nutrients of sugar cane juice and is made without additional chemicals. You have to go to a health food store or on the Internet to find it. It has a heavenly flavor and a low GI rating, so is ideal for baking, sprinkling over breakfast cereals, and so on, and for replacing light brown sugar in your cooking.

MANGO AND PASSION FRUIT

Passion fruits often look rather wrinkled—that's perfectly normal.
The secret is to choose fruits that feel heavy.

serves 4

2–3 large ripe mangos
8 passion fruits

Slice the mangos down each side of the flat pit, as close as you can to the pit. Remove the peel, slice the flesh, and lay the pieces in a shallow dish or plate.

Halve the passion fruit and scoop the pulp and seeds over the mango. Leave for at least 30 minutes before serving, to allow the fragrant flavors to mingle.

ORANGES AND PASSION FRUIT The colors are similar, the flavors different, in this variation. Use 6 large oranges instead of the mangos. Hold an orange over a bowl and, with a sharp knife, cut off the peel, removing the white parts as well, cutting around and around, as if you were trying to take the peel off in one long curl. Repeat for the remaining oranges. Then, either slice the oranges into thin rounds or cut the juicy segments away from the skin and white parts. Cover with passion fruit pulp as above.

PERSIMMONS OR SHARON FRUIT If you can find these at just the right point of ripeness—that is, very ripe indeed without having gone too far—they're divine. Just peel, chop, and serve as above.

LYCHEES, KIWIS, AND GINGER

This is a very refreshing mixture that I love to eat after spicy dishes.
I tend, rather lazily, to use canned lychees, which I find fragrant and
delicious, but fresh ones would be even nicer if you have the patience
to peel off the hard skins.

serves 4–6

> 2 × 1¾ cups (400 g) canned lychees
> 4 kiwi fruits
> 4 pieces bottled preserved ginger
> 4 tablespoons ginger syrup

Drain the lychees and rinse under cold running water to remove the syrup. Arrange the lychees on a
serving platter. Peel the kiwis and slice into thin rounds or segments. Chop the preserved ginger roughly.
Add the kiwis and ginger to the platter and pour the ginger syrup over them. Mix lightly and serve.

APRICOT AND ORANGE FOOL WITH PISTACHIOS

This is a lovely sweet whip. You do need to allow the apricots time to
soak, but then it's just a question of process and serve. It's essential to
use organic apricots for this recipe.

serves 4–6

> 1 cup (250 g) organic whole dried apricots (see page 168)
> juice of 4 oranges
> 1 cup (250 g) firm or silken tofu, drained and broken into pieces
> ½ cup (125 ml) soy creamer (see page 169)
> 6–8 cardamoms, pods discarded, seeds crushed (optional)
> 2 tablespoons (25 g) pistachio nuts, shelled and chopped

Soak the apricots in the orange juice for several hours—overnight if possible. Then process to a paste.

Add the tofu, soy creamer, and crushed cardamoms, if using, and process again to make a smooth, thick
cream. Spoon into individual dessert glasses and sprinkle with the nuts.

DRIED FRUIT COMPOTE

This is popular in the Middle East and there are lots of variations. You can use different mixtures of dried fruits—soak them in water or fruit juice, then cook them or leave them as they are. If you choose to cook them, you can add spices, such as a piece of cinnamon stick, a little grated fresh ginger, or some crushed cardamom pods. When the compote is done, you can add pieces of fresh fruit and flaked or whole blanched almonds, or crushed pistachios. You can also make an intensely iron-rich version by adding 1 tablespoon of blackstrap molasses to the soaking liquid—this is useful as a pick-me-up and for iron boosting (see page 19). This compote can be served as a snack, as a dessert, or for breakfast, with cream, soy creamer, or thick yogurt.

serves 4

½ cup (115 g) each of organic dried figs, apricots, or peaches, dates, yellow raisins, and prunes (about 2 cups/450 g in total of whatever mixture you fancy)
water, apple juice, or orange juice, to cover
4 tablespoons (50 g) almonds, flaked or blanched, or pistachios, shelled and chopped

Wash the fruit and put it into a bowl. Cover completely with water or fruit juice and leave to stand for several hours—24 hours isn't too long as it just goes on getting better. Or you could soak the fruit for a few hours, then simmer it for 20–30 minutes until very tender. If you're doing this, I think it's best to use water rather than fruit juice for soaking.

Serve warm or cold with the nuts mixed in or scattered on top.

ORGANIC DRIED APRICOTS If you've never tasted organic dried apricots, which are a modest-looking, mousy brown, you've no idea of the treat in store for you. They have the most wonderful, sweet, brown-sugary flavor. Eat them straight from the package—they make a healthy treat for children. Use them in the compote above, in the Apricot and Orange Fool with Pistachios on page 166, or simply make them into a paste by soaking (or lightly cooking) in water, then puréeing. Spoon this over yogurt, spread on bread, or eat as it is. Try the Hunza apricots, which look like pebbles in the bag, but taste divine if you cover them with water and soak for a few hours, then cook gently for 15–20 minutes, or until they are tender and the liquid is syrupy. Alternatively you could eat them just as they are.

MULLED WINE PEARS

A spicy version of an old favorite. They're delightful on their own, or with yogurt, soy creamer (*see below*), or ice cream and maybe some fancy cookies if you really want to do it in style.

serves 6

6 firm dessert pears
6 tablespoons (85 g) fructose (*see page 164*) or superfine sugar
1¾ cups (400 ml) red wine
grated zest of 1 organic orange
2 star anise
a few drops of red vegetable coloring (optional)
2 tablespoons preserved ginger in syrup, finely chopped

Peel the pears, leaving them whole and reserving the stalks. Put the sugar into a saucepan with the wine, orange zest, 1¾ cups (400 ml) water, and the star anise, and heat gently until the sugar has dissolved, then bring to the boil.

Add the pears, cover the pan, and simmer gently for 30–40 minutes, or until the pears are tender right through to the center. If they look little drab, enhance them with a few drops of vegetable coloring, if you like.

With a slotted spoon, transfer the pears from the pan to a serving dish. Add the ginger to the pan and boil vigorously until the liquid has reduced and looks shiny, then pour this over the pears. Make sure the pretty star anise are visible.

Serve at room temperature with a bowl of whipped cream, a jug of soy creamer, or a bowl of ice cream.

VEGAN "CREAM" Soy creamer is sold in a vacuum pack, has the appearance and consistency of light cream, and a creamy, rather sweet flavor. You can use it in all the ways you would use light cream. If you want a thicker cream for spooning, simply pour it into a small saucepan and boil it gently, uncovered, until it has reduced by about half. Cool, then use as required—it's delicious with the Mulled Wine Pears (*see above*), for instance. For a sharper "sour cream" version, simply stir in 1 teaspoon or so of lemon juice, which will thicken it even more and also add sharpness.

HONEY AND CINNAMON-ROASTED FIGS

In the summer, there's nothing to beat warm, sun-ripened figs, and nothing to do to them except eat them. However, when you can't get them, here is a way to make less-than-perfect fresh figs really heavenly.

serves 4

12 figs
3 tablespoons clear honey
2–3 teaspoons cinnamon
thick Greek-style yogurt, to serve

Preheat the oven to 400°F (200°C), or heat the broiler.

Cut a cross in the top of each fig, piercing through the stem but not right through the base, so that the pieces remain intact. Put them into a shallow ovenproof dish, pulling them open gently as you do. Drizzle the honey over the insides of the figs and sprinkle with cinnamon.

Bake or broil for about 15 minutes, or until the figs are tender and fragrant but not collapsed. Serve with thick Greek-style yogurt.

HONEY AND CINNAMON-ROASTED PLUMS For this delicious variation, halve and pit 3 cups (750 g) plums—it doesn't matter if they're hard. Put them into an ovenproof dish with the honey and cinnamon and cook as above, until tender.

FOR A VEGAN ALTERNATIVE, use agave syrup, brown rice syrup, or apple juice concentrate instead of the honey.

EXOTIC FRUIT COMPOTE WITH COCONUT CREAM

If you can get fresh lychees, and have the time to peel off their hard
skin and pit them, then use them; otherwise, canned lychees are fine.
Make sure all the fruit is ripe—buy it a few days in advance if necessary.

serves 4

FOR THE COCONUT CREAM
7-ounce (200-g) block creamed coconut
grated rind of I lemon or lime
  or ½ teaspoon real vanilla extract (optional)
a little honey, agave syrup, or apple juice concentrate
  (see page 164), for sweetening (optional)

2 tablespoons clear honey
juice of 2 oranges
I ripe mango
I small papaya
2 kiwi fruit
I cup (250 g) black grapes
2 cups (425 g) canned lychees, drained
4 passion fruit

Start by making the coconut cream, so that it has time to cool. Cut the creamed coconut block into small pieces and put in a bowl set over a pan of steaming water. Add 6 tablespoons boiling water to the coconut and leave for a few minutes to melt, then stir until smooth and creamy. Add the lemon or lime zest, or the vanilla extract (real vanilla tastes great but darkens the cream slightly), and sweeten to taste —I find it sweet enough as it is. Leave to cool.

Make a fresh syrup by mixing the honey and orange juice in a large bowl.

Cut the mango down each side of the flat pit, as close as you can to the pit. Remove the peel, slice the flesh into chunks, and add them to the bowl.

Peel the papaya, remove the seeds, and slice the flesh. Peel and slice the kiwi fruit. Add these to the bowl, along with the grapes, halved and seeded if necessary, and the lychees.

Just before you want to serve the compote, halve the passion fruit, scoop out all the juice and seeds, and add to the rest of the fruit. Stir gently, then serve with the cooled coconut cream.

FRUITS, SUGAR, AND SPICE

PEACH AND BLUEBERRY COMPOTE

Another really simple recipe—but such a winner, in my opinion. (And did you know that blueberries help retard the aging process?) The fructose (or superfine sugar) is optional—for more about fructose, see page 164.

serves 4

4 peaches, washed, pitted and thinly sliced
2½ cups (500 g) blueberries, washed
4 tablespoons apple juice concentrate (*see page 164*)
4 tablespoons fructose or superfine sugar (optional)

Put the peaches and blueberries into a saucepan with the apple juice concentrate and fructose or superfine sugar, if using—it might not be necessary if the fruit is really sweet. Heat gently for 5–10 minutes, until the juices run and the peaches are just tender. Serve warm or cold.

VANILLA-POACHED PEACHES WITH ALMONDS Using 6–7 peaches instead of the peaches and blueberries, prepare the compote as above, adding 2 vanilla pods, broken in half. Cook until the peaches are tender, then add 3 tablespoons whole blanched almonds.

BLACKBERRY AND APPLE COMPOTE Use 4 eating apples, peeled and sliced, and 4 cups (500 g) blackberries instead of the peaches and blueberries. Put them into a pan with the apple juice concentrate and fructose or superfine sugar, if using, and cook gently, with a lid on the pan, for 15–20 minutes, or until the apples are tender to the point of a knife. Serve warm or cold.

SUMMER BERRY COMPOTE Make as above, using 6 cups (750 g) mixed summer berries—strawberries, loganberries, blueberries, raspberries. Remove stalks, and halve or quarter larger strawberries. Heat gently with the apple juice concentrate and fructose or superfine sugar, if using, until the juices run. If you're using loganberries, you may need to add a little more fructose or superfine sugar.

SEASONAL CELEBRATIONS

SPRING

Green Pea Soup with Mint (*see page 28*)

Saffron Risotto Cake with Red Bell Peppers (*see page 134*)

Braised Vegetables with Lemon and Parsley (*see page 31*)

Chocolate Mousse Cake (*see page 187*)
  or Chocolate Vegan Victoria Sandwich Cake (*see page 186*)

SUMMER

Baba Ghanouj (*see page 87*) with raw vegetables

Roasted Vegetable and Goat Cheese Torte or vegan variation (*see page 48*)

Bean Salad Niçoise (*see page 89*)

Little Gem, Belgian Endive, and Watercress Salad (*see page 33*)

Sparkling Raspberry Jello (*see page 181*)

FALL

WINTER

CARDAMOM AND ROSE ICE CREAM

This ice cream is wonderful and is actually vegan, though everyone finds that difficult to believe. It's best if you can make it in an ice-cream maker —I have one of those inexpensive ones where you keep the bowl in the freezer, and it's so useful for this recipe. You can buy soy creamer at any health food store and at some supermarkets.

serves 4

2 cups (2 x 250-ml cartons) of soy creamer (*see page 169*)
8–10 cardamom pods, lightly crushed
1 vanilla pod
⅔ cup (140 g) fructose (*see page 164*) or superfine sugar
1 tablespoon rosewater
4 tablespoons (50 g) pistachio nuts, shelled and roughly chopped

Put the soy creamer into a pan with the cardamom pods and vanilla pod and bring just to the boil, then remove from the heat, cover, and leave for as long as you can—at least 10 minutes, or until it's cold, if you have time—for the flavors to mingle.

Strain the cream into a bowl, pressing the cardamom against the sieve to make sure you extract every last bit of flavor. If you feel like making it really special, split the vanilla pod, scrape out the black seeds, and add to the cream. Or just remove the vanilla pod, rinse, and let it dry to use again.

Stir the fructose or superfine sugar, the rosewater, and pistachio nuts into the cream, then pour into an ice-cream maker and "churn" until thick. Or pour into a shallow container and place in the freezer, whisking a couple of times during freezing as the mixture starts to solidify, to make it as smooth as possible.

CARAMEL AND WALNUT ICE CREAM Make as above using ⅔ cup (140 g) rapadura sugar (*see page 164*)—which gives a wonderful caramelized flavor—or light brown sugar, instead of the fructose or superfine sugar. Omit the cardamom, vanilla, and rosewater, and use chopped walnuts instead of pistachio nuts.

CARAMEL AND CHOCOLATE CHIP ICE CREAM Follow the Caramel and Walnut Ice Cream recipe, but use 4 tablespoons (50 g) dark (vegan) chocolate chips or diced plain (vegan) chocolate instead of the nuts.

SPICY APRICOT FLAPJACKS

Everyone loves these and they're so easy to make—and relatively healthy too, if you use canola oil, which isn't as likely to be damaged at high temperatures as other oils. If you can get rapadura sugar (available from the best health food stores), use it for this recipe, because it has a lower GI rating than other sugars and a wonderful caramel flavor. Otherwise use a light brown sugar.

makes 20 pieces

½ cup (125 ml) canola oil
⅔ cup (140 g) rapadura sugar (*see page 164*) or light brown sugar
2 scant cups (200 g) rolled oats
4 tablespoons (50 g) brazil nuts, chopped
2 tablespoons (50 g) dried apricots, chopped
½ teaspoon ground ginger
pinch of ground cinnamon
1–2 pinches of chili pepper flakes or powder
2 teaspoons agave syrup (*see page 164*) or extra water

Preheat the oven to 400°F (200°C).

Simply mix all the ingredients together and press into a lightly oiled 11 x 9-inch (19 x 29-cm) jelly roll pan. Bake for 10 minutes, or until golden brown. Cool in the pan but mark into slices while the mixture is still warm. The mixture is quite crumbly so don't try to remove the flapjack pieces from the pan until they're completely cold, and use a spatula to do so.

FLAPJACK VARIATIONS You can vary the dried fruit and nuts used—chopped dried peaches are good, as are raisins or yellow raisins. If you're making them for young children, you might like to leave out the nuts or use sunflower, pumpkin or sesame seeds. Plain flapjacks, without either nuts or dried fruit, also work well. For a particularly nutritious (but strong-tasting) version, replace the syrup with 1 tablespoon (or more) of blackstrap molasses.

FRUITS, SUGAR, AND SPICE

SPARKLING RASPBERRY JELLO

The best kind of vegetarian gelatin to use is agar flakes (*see below*). You just sprinkle these over cold liquid, then heat gently until all the flakes have dissolved. Measure the flakes carefully—the amount given makes a soft jello that you can easily get your spoon into (approximately 2 teaspoons of agar flakes to 1 scant cup (200 ml) liquid). For a firmer jello, you could increase the amount to 12 teaspoons for this recipe, but I wouldn't use any more than this or you end up with something too tough and bouncy.

serves 4–6

3 cups (750 ml) white grape juice
8 teaspoons agar flakes
⅔ cup (140 g) raspberries

Pour the grape juice into a saucepan. Sprinkle the agar flakes on top—don't stir—and heat gently for about 5 minutes, or until the flakes have dissolved. Then bring to the boil, remove from the heat, and set aside to cool briefly.

Meanwhile, divide the raspberries between 4–6 sundae glasses or deep wineglasses. Pour the warm grape juice over the raspberries. Leave to cool, then chill in the refrigerator.

AGAR This is a vegetarian "gelatin" made from seaweed. I prefer to use the natural flakes that are a transparent whitish color. These can be found in health food stores. They're quite simple to use (*see above*), but they need a little care because you can't just use them in the same way you would gelatin.

STICKY PARKIN

This perennial favorite will keep in an airtight container for 7–10 days and it just goes on getting more and more deliciously sticky.

makes 12–16 pieces

4 tablespoons canola oil
6 tablespoons (175 g) blackstrap molasses
8 tablespoons agave syrup, apple juice concentrate,
  or brown rice syrup (see page 164)
½ cup (115 g) rapadura sugar (see page 164) or light brown sugar
½ cup (115 g) whole wheat pastry flour
2 teaspoons baking powder
1 tablespoon ground ginger
1 cup (115 g) medium rolled oats
6 tablespoons soy milk

Preheat the oven to 325°F (160°C). Line an 8-inch (20-cm) square pan with nonstick baking parchment.

Put the canola oil, blackstrap molasses (if you dip the spoon into the canola oil first, the molasses will slither off the spoon easily), your chosen syrup, and sugar into a saucepan and heat gently until melted.

Put the whole wheat flour, baking powder, ginger, and oatmeal into a bowl. Stir the soy milk into the melted ingredients, which will cool them down, then pour the mixture on top of the dry ingredients and mix together quickly.

Pour the mixture into the prepared pan and bake for 50–60 minutes, or until it springs back when pressed lightly in the center. Cool in the pan, then cut into pieces.

STICKY DATE BREAD

This is a dark, moist bread studded with sweet, gooey pieces of date.
Serve in thick slices, spread with a little butter if you like.

makes 1 loaf

**2 tablespoons agave syrup, apple juice concentrate,
 or brown rice syrup (see page 164)**
4 tablespoons blackstrap molasses
5 tablespoons soy milk
4 tablespoons rapeseed oil
2 cups (225 g) barley flour or whole wheat flour
1 teaspoon pumpkin pie spice
1 teaspoon baking powder
2 tablespoons (50 g) rapadura sugar (see page 164) or light brown sugar
½ cup (115 g) pitted dates, chopped

Preheat the oven to 375°F (190°C). Line a 1-pound (450-g) loaf pan with a long strip of nonstick baking paper or greased parchment paper to cover the base and the narrow sides.

Heat your chosen syrup, blackstrap molasses, and the soy milk gently in a saucepan until dissolved, then stir in the oil, remove from the heat, and set aside.

Put the barley flour, mixed spice, baking powder, your chosen sugar, and the dates into a bowl. Pour in the melted syrup mixture and stir until combined. Spoon into the prepared pan and bake for 50–60 minutes, or until the top is firm to a light touch and a skewer inserted into the center comes out clean.

Cool in the pan, then unmold onto a cake rack and peel off the paper.

LEMON CAKE

This is a beautiful moist golden cake with an intense lemon flavor.
It contains no flour and is perfect to serve with a berry or other fruit
compote (I particularly like it with the Summer Berry Compote on page
175), or to eat on its own. You need an electric whisk to make this cake.

makes 1 cake

2 lemons, unwaxed, preferably organic
6 eggs
1 scant cup (200 g) fructose (*see page 164*) or superfine sugar
2 cups (250 g) ground almonds

Preheat the oven to 300°F (150°C). Line an 8-inch (20-cm) round cake pan—preferably a springform or one with a loose base—with nonstick baking parchment.

Wash the lemons, then put them into a pan, cover with water, and bring to the boil. Leave to cook gently for about 45 minutes, or until the lemons are very tender when tested with a sharp knife. Leave to cool.

Drain the lemons and cut them open so you can remove any seeds. Then put the lemons into a food processor and process to a golden paste.

Whisk the eggs and sugar together for about 5 minutes until they are pale and very thick, and until a little of the mixture, flicked on top of the rest, will hold its shape for a few seconds.

Whisk in the lemon paste, then fold in the ground almonds, using a metal spoon.

Pour the mixture into the pan and bake for 1¼ hours, or until a cocktail stick inserted into the center of the cake comes out clean. If it starts to get too brown, cover lightly with a piece of nonstick baking parchment. Cool the cake in the pan, then unmold carefully, and remove the paper.

VEGAN VICTORIA SANDWICH CAKE

This is a delightful cake; the orange makes it a pretty pale gold color, and adds a delicate flavor which goes well with the raspberry jelly. The consistency is light and moist—no one would guess there were no eggs in this cake unless you told them.

makes 1 cake

1½ cups (175 g) organic white self-rising flour
3 teaspoons baking powder
6 tablespoons (3 oz) fructose (*see page 164*) or superfine sugar
½ cup (4 oz) ground almonds
grated rind of 1 orange
juice of 1 orange, made up to 1¼ cups (300 ml) with water
6 tablespoons canola oil

FOR THE FILLING AND TOPPING
2 tablespoons all-fruit raspberry jelly
a little fructose or superfine sugar, for sprinkling

Preheat the oven to 350°F (180°C). Line the bases of 2 × 8-inch (20-cm) shallow cake pans with nonstick baking parchment.

Put the flour, baking powder, fructose or superfine sugar, ground almonds, and grated orange rind into a large bowl and mix, then add the orange juice-and-water mixture and the oil, and mix well.

Divide the mixture between the 2 pans and bake for 20 minutes, or until the tops of the cakes spring back when lightly pressed.

Leave to cool in the pans, then remove, and strip off the paper. Sandwich the cakes together with the jelly, and sprinkle a little fructose or superfine sugar on top of the cake.

CHOCOLATE VEGAN VICTORIA SANDWICH CAKE For this delectable variation, replace 4 tablespoons (50 g) of the flour with the same quantity of good-quality unsweetened cocoa powder. The grated orange rind is optional, but keep the juice as this helps the cake to rise. Sandwich the cakes with all-fruit black cherry jelly, or a chocolate cream made by beating 6 tablespoons (85 g) good-quality vegan margarine with 6 tablespoons (85 g) fructose or powdered (confectioner's) sugar, 2 tablespoons cocoa powder, and 1 teaspoon of vanilla extract, until light and fluffy. Dust the top of the cake with fructose or powdered (confectioner's) sugar.

CHOCOLATE MOUSSE CAKE

This is one of those chocolate cakes made without flour. Warm from the oven and still molten in the center, this makes a perfect "pudding cake" for a special treat, and is one of the few occasions these days when I'll eat a little cream, lightly whipped and cold from the refrigerator, which blends voluptuously with the warm, oozing chocolate. When cold, it also makes a wonderful celebration cake, densely chocolatey and gooey. It needs no adornment, except possibly a sprinkling of sugar.

makes 1 cake

I pound (450 g) semisweet chocolate
½ cup (115 g) butter, cut into pieces
6 free-range eggs
½ cup (115 g) fructose, rapadura sugar (see page 164),
   light brown sugar, or superfine sugar
I tablespoon pure vanilla extract
a little fructose or powdered (confectioner's) sugar to sprinkle (optional)

Preheat the oven to 350°F (180°C). Line an 8-inch (20-cm) round cake pan—preferably a springform or one with a loose base—with nonstick baking parchment.

Break the chocolate into pieces and put into a heatproof glass or ceramic bowl with the butter. Set it over a pan of gently steaming water and leave to melt.

Meanwhile, separate the eggs. Whisk the whites until stiff. Reserve them while you whisk together the yolks and sugar (no need to wash the whisk in between) until they're thick and pale.

Whisk the melted chocolate mixture in with the egg yolks, along with the vanilla extract, then, using a metal spoon, fold in the egg whites.

Tip the mixture into the prepared pan and bake for 25 minutes until set but still liquid in the center. If you want a firmer center, cook it for 5–10 minutes longer. Cool in the pan. Remove the paper carefully before serving, and sprinkle with a little fructose or powdered (confectioner's) sugar, if using.

NOTES ON INGREDIENTS

Agave syrup You can get this from health food stores and from good Mexican grocery stores.

Amaranth and popped amaranth Available from health food stores and by mail order.

Apple cider vinegar (organic) Try to find the best quality from health food stores or by mail order.

Apple juice concentrate Several good brands are available from health food stores; make sure you buy organic.

Apricots, organic, including Hunza apricots Available from good health food stores and by mail order.

Arrowroot Available from specialty stores, health food stores, and some supermarkets.

Barley, organic pearl Order from health food stores, such as Whole Foods Market, Inc., Austin, Texas.

Blackstrap molasses You can find this in any supermarket and health food store.

Brown rice syrup Available from good health food stores.

Buckwheat Natural, untoasted buckwheat can be found in most health food stores and in grocery stores in neighborhoods with a large Russian population.

Creamed coconut, coconut milk, and coconut butter Creamed coconut and coconut milk are available from supermarkets, health food stores, as well as southeast Asian grocery stores. The best coconut butter is made by Omega Nutrition, and can be found in nutrition centers or ordered direct by mail order from:

Omega Nutrition
6515 Aldrich Rd.
Bellingham WA 98226
Tel: (800) 661-FLAX (3529)
Fax: (604) 253-4228
Website: www.omeganutrution.com

Curry leaves, fresh Available from any ethnic East Indian food stores, if you're lucky enough to live near one. Otherwise from specialty and gourmet food stores.

Epazote Easy to find in any Mexican grocery store and supermarkets in Mexican neighborhoods.

Flaxseed oil Order from good quality health food stores or from Omega Nutrition (*see under* coconut butter above).

Flours Whole wheat flour and spelt flours are available from most good health food stores and many supermarkets. For chickpea (gram) flour, also known as garbanzo flour or besan, visit a Mexican or East Indian grocery store, or try mail order through the Internet.

Green soybeans (edamame) Buy these frozen from Chinese or Japanese grocery stores.

Kuzu Available from Japanese and gourmet grocery stores.

Flaxseeds Best to buy these whole, and grind them yourself. They are quite widely available from most health food stores.

Mirin Available from Japanese and gourmet grocery stores.

Miso Organic whole barley miso is available from nutrition centers and health food stores.

Muesli Muesli is available from good health food and gourmet stores.

Nut butters A huge variety of nut butters is now available from health food stores, including almond, pecan, cashew, and macadamia. When buying peanut butter, make sure it's organic and contains no sugar or palm oil.

Nutritional yeast flakes Engevita nutritional yeast flakes are available from good health food stores.

Olive oil, unfiltered cold-pressed organic Most of these oils are from California and are stocked in all gourmet and health food stores.

Quinoa and popped quinoa Available from Mexican and health food stores.

Rapadura sugar Available from good health food stores.

Rice vinegar Available from good health food stores and Japanese grocery stores.

Sea vegetables and agar flakes Now available in some supermarkets and most good health food stores as well as all Japanese grocery stores.

Seitan Lightlife makes seitan, tempeh, and many other grain and soy products. To find your nearest outlet, contact Lightlife Foods, 153 Industrial Boulevard, Turners Falls, MA 01376, or email them at info@lightlife.com.

Soy sauce Kikkoman is available from any supermarket and from Japanese stores. Tamari can be found at good health food stores.

Soy natural garlic and parsley pasta This "alternative" pasta is made by an Australian company called Orgran. It can be bought by mail order.

Soy yogurt, soy milk, and soy creamer Up Country Organics of Vermont make a natural live organic soy yogurt—buy it from good health food stores. The Tofu Shop (see below under tofu) also makes these. Soy creamer is available from any health food store and many supermarkets.

Tahini Be sure to buy the light one as dark tahini is rather bitter. Available from health food and Middle Eastern grocery stores where it is also known as tahina.

Tempeh Available from southeast Asian and specialty health food stores and from Lightlife Foods, 153, Industrial Boulevard, Turners Falls, MA 01376. info@lightlife.com

Tofu Among the many suppliers of tofu products in the United States is the Tofu Shop, 65 Frank Martin Court, Arcata, CA 95521. Tel: (707) 822 7401. info@tofushop.com. There are many other tofu makers; shop around and see which variety you like best.

Cellophane noodles Also known as glass noodles, these can be found in any Chinese or Japanese supermarket, but you probably won't be able to read the package. Health food stores sell mung bean pasta.

Unrefined salt You can buy this in gourmet food stores in the United States, since Morton Salt owns one of the biggest French salt producers, but it can also be ordered direct from France.

A FEW USEFUL BOOKS

Cox, Peter, *The Realeat Encyclopaedia of Vegetarian Living*, Bloomsbury Books, UK, 1994

Elliot, Rose, *Mother, Baby and Toddler Book*, Collins, UK, 1996

Foster-Powell, Kaye; Brand-Miller, Jenny; and Wolever, Thomas, *The Glucose Revolution Pocket Guide to the Top 100 Low Glycemic Foods*, Marlowe & Company, Tucson AZ, 2000

Janogly, Lee, *Stop Bingeing!*, Elliot Right Way Books, UK, 2000

Lacombe, Isabelle, *Michel Montignac's Recipes and Menus Adapted for North America*, Michel-Ange Publishing, NY, 2003

Montignac, Michel, *Eat Yourself Slim Cookbook*, Erica House Book Publishing, Baltimore, MD, 1999

Spencer, Colin, *Vegetarianism, A History*, Four Walls, Eight Windows, NY, 2001

Willcox (M.D.), Bradley; Willcox (Ph.D.), Craig; and Suzuki (M.D.), Makoto, *The Okinawa Program*, Three Rivers Press, New York, 2002

Woollams, Chris, *Everything You Need to Know to Help You Beat Cancer*, Health Issues, UK, 2002

ORGANIZATIONS

North American Vegetarian Society (NAVS)
P.O. Box 72,
Dolgeville, NY 13329
Navs@telenet.net

The American Vegan Society
56 Dinshah Lane, P.O. Box 369,
Malaga NJ 08328 Tel: (856) 694-2887
Fax: (856) 694-2288 Hosted by
www.vegsource.com,
www.americanvegan.org

Viva! (Vegetarian International Voice for Animals)
Viva! USA
P.O. Box 4398
Davis, CA 95617
Tel: (530) 759-viva (8482)
Fax: (530) 759-8487
Email: info@vivausa.org

Viva! in the USA publishes *Vegan Basics*, a guide to all the vegan resources in the U.S., which also provides information on what commercial products happen to be vegan "by accident" such as Dreyers' Edys sorbets. The guide is free, but Viva! would appreciate a donation.

The Vegan Society This, the world's first vegan society, is "seeking ways of living free from the use of animal products for the benefit of people, animals and the environment" and provides facts on many topics, including nutrition and health. Tel: +44 (0)1424 427393, www.vegansociety.com

OMEGA-3 SUPPLEMENTS

www.healthfind.org is a web portal that will take you to a number of sites that offer Omega-3 supplements by mail order.

Superfood, a wonderful nutritional supplement made from completely natural ingredients and packed with vitamins and, most important, vegetarian sources of long-chain omega-3 oils, made by leading herbalist Dr. Richard Schulze, founder of the American Botanical Pharmacy. For availability of this and other American Botanical Pharmacy products, contact Dr. Richard Schultze, P.O. Box 3628 Santa Monica, CA 90408, Tel: (310)576-6565, Fax: (310) 576-6575.

DHA Gold capsules Available from supermarkets and pharmacies. www.dhadepot.com

Neuromins capsules Available from supermarkets and pharmacies. www.martekbio.com

Index

Page numbers in *italics* refer to illustrations